END TO END
ON THE
HORSE-SHOE TRAIL

Hiking the Horse-Shoe Trail
from Valley Forge
to the Appalachian Trail.

MICHAEL D. PAVELEK, II

i

Pavelek Publishing Company
863 Tallyho Drive
Hershey, PA 17033

First Edition, 2000

Text Design by John Marcucci, P&J Printing, Inc., Hershey, PA, 17033.

Cover Design by Roy Spancake, P&J Printing, Inc., Hershey, PA, 17033.

Cover Photo of the Author by Michael D. Pavelek, III, Bowie, MD.

Poem in introduction by Stephen F. Taylor, Alexandria, VA,
used with permission.

Printed by P&J Printing, Inc., Hershey, PA, 17033.

Manufactured in Pennsylvania, USA

ISBN 0-9677503-0-X
Library of Congress Card Number: 00-191187

First Printing, April 2000.

END TO END ON THE HORSE-SHOE TRAIL

Table of Contents

Dedication

This book is dedicated to the people who established and maintain the Horse-Shoe Trail, and to the many individuals and organizations who have provided a corridor for this trail to cross their property. Thank you for your hospitality.

With appreciation to:

Diane Pavelek, my wife, who supported me in walking the Horse-Shoe Trail through drop offs, pick ups, babysitting our grandson so our children (natural and in law) could hike with me, and in the writing of this book.

Michael Pavelek III, Ann Daube Pavelek and Renee Pavelek for hiking with me and waiting for me on the hills, as well as for their thoughts and support on the trail.

Larry Taylor, for his support in getting ready for the hike, advice on equipment, company in completing the "loose ends" and finishing the hike, and for the example he sets for the Scouts he mentors.

Stephen F. Taylor for permission to use his poem.

John Marcucci of P&J Printing, Inc, Hershey, PA, for finding a way to publish the manuscript.

And the hundreds of people I met along the trail who provided refreshments, encouragement, a pleasant greeting, directions, permission to cross their property, places to park my vehicle or bicycle, and use of their phone to call home.

Thank you all, this has been a very positive experience.
MICHAEL D. PAVELEK II

Introduction

"Take a Hike!" Is there significance in this common statement? As Renee's friend, Stephen Taylor, wrote on the inside cover of her trail log before she departed for our hike:

"Take it all in
Discover it
Feel it
Embrace it
Never Forget!"

–Stephen F. Taylor,
Alexandria, VA

This is the story of what I saw and experienced on the Horse-Shoe Trail. It was written to motivate you to share this experience in the hope that you will take this hike. After hiking the Horse-Shoe Trail you will have a perspecctive which provides a good insight on the value of walking trails as a community and recreational resource. You will also understand the environmental and social challenges trails face. Perhaps, you will see enough value in the Horse-Shoe Trail that you will actively support purchase and integration of land for the Horse-Shoe Trail corridor to pass through our rapidly developing communities. Perhaps, you will come to view walking trails as a necessary and integral part of land use and planning programs in your community's development.

Mike Pavelek, II,
Hershey, PA
November, 1999.

Chapter
1

There Is More Than
One Way to Take a Hike!

Whether you plan to hike from end to end - through hiking - on a remote wilderness trail, hike a circuit trail at a state park, or hike one or more sections of the more than 2,000 miles of available trails in Pennsylvania, you will rapidly learn that there is more than one way to take a hike.

Numerous literature exists on the challenges and preparations for through hiking the longer trails. Completion of the trails over 300 miles or so requires a commitment of time, the willingness to embrace the demanding physical exertion and acceptance of spartan living conditions. Even with a support team dedicated to your hike, which many of us simply cannot afford or possibly do not desire, it is important to be prepared for real contingencies - such as being lost.

The ease and convenience of starting from home and calling on the cellular phone for a ride diminishes with increasing distance from your home. One gradually learns through experience the advantages and disadvantages of the numerous methods of conducting a hike. In addition, there are different levels of convenience, physical exertion and cash expense associated with each method. In one case, personal physical safety became a serious concern (See White Out on the Horse Shoe Trail, Chapter 5) and resulted in a decision to turn back and try again another day.

The most convenient, safe and inexpensive hikes were those close to my home. During the first two days of hiking, home was always within easy walking distance. Shelter, food and water were virtually assured due to the number of 24 hour commercial establishments in the area and the the fact that the cellular phone worked. If family was not available I could count on a friend for a ride home. Because of these factors and given that the trail changes daily, especially with the seasons, these hikes will probably be often repeated either alone or with friends.

Further away from home (first to the north and west), logistical challenges encountered educated me concerning various Civil War battles in the Shenandoah Valley I had read about. If the armies of the 1860's had to travel around the mountains, to stay on passable roads and thus transport their supplies, several more days could be required to reach a point over one mountain which did not have a road. During the 1860's and today, there are only three major accesses through the Appalachian Mountains on the entire length of the Skyline Drive through Virginia. This lesson was made very clear when I tried to reach the access to the Horse-Shoe Trail, east of the town of Dauphin, Pennsylvania.

By vehicle, from Hershey, PA, it was necessary to travel by road another 30 plus miles to hike the ten or so miles between Stony Valley and Manada Gap Road. It may be faster to cross the Stony Mountain area on foot at two or three miles per hour than to drive around on current roads at 50 miles per hour! Armies in 1860 didn't move at 50 miles per hour!

Cost is another issue. Hiking alone and depending on a second vehicle for pick up results in about 120 miles of vehicle travel. Sixty miles for the first vehicle to go and return, and another sixty miles for the second vehicle to retrieve the hikers, drop them off at the starting point so that they could walk to the first vehicle then return. All of this to hike only ten miles. The ratio of drive to hike becomes exorbitant and expensive.

I soon learned that other methods of access and return, such as hiking longer distances between pick up points, or taking two vehicles and more hikers, was more effective. Changing keys at the mid point so that each group of hikers, walking in opposite directions, could pool a vehicle would also be more effective for larger groups.

One lesson, which was learned again and again, was the value of a good map and a functional compass. The value of these items was reinforced each time the trail was not obvious for various reasons, or the hiker was watching scenery and wandered away from the trail of blazes (the 4 centimeter by 15 centimeter colored, rectangular markings which indicate the trail route), becoming lost. The map and compass are essential tools for all but short walks. Don't leave home without them!

Taking time off from work to hike longer segments at one time and carrying all of the materials needed in a pack may be expensive in terms of value of vacation time and certainly is much more physically demanding. How you choose to do your hikes must be based on your preferences, resources, convenience, and choices of company, time, transportation, etc. Another lesson I learned is that if hiking the entire trail is the objective, one should not develop too many "loose ends." Loose ends are the areas of trail which are not connected to completed segments. (This is described in Chapter 21, Tick Infested.) I don't profess to suggest what you do, but I do encourage that you do pay attention to matters of logistics, finding your way, and safety. Failure to properly plan for necessary items in the more remote areas or to use some discretion, may have unfortunate results, spoil your hike or ride, or result in injury. Being injured or lost will cause stressful situations both for you and those others who may actually care about your whereabouts and well being more than you do. Be considerate of your family, friends, and those who will be called upon to rescue you. Tell someone where you are, when you plan to be back, the route you are taking, and take care of yourself. As I found, to my dismay, the cellular phone does not always work to call for a ride, or for help!

Methods of getting to and from the trail experienced were:

Hike from home and call for pick up. Map 8, Chapters 2 and 3.

Drop off and hike home. Map 9, Chapter 4.

Drop off and hike to staged vehicle. Map 9, Chapter 4, 5, 6. Also Map 6, Chapter 10.

Leap Frogging Vehicles. Map 1,2, Chapters 11, 12, 13.

Park, Hike and Hope - Parking the vehicle at the origin, hiking to a pick up point, and hoping that your ride shows up and that you reach the same point near the same time. (A disaster for me.) See Chapter 15, Lost, Confused and Frustrated.

A variation of the Park, Hike and Hope was the drop off and then pick up the hiker later. Map 7, Chapter 2. This method was also used on longer hikes, say two or three days, on other trails. The advantage is not worrying about the vehicles. The disadvantages are rushing to make the designated pick up time and place, waiting for the ride or hikers to show up, or being at the wrong pick up point.

Park, Bicycle, Hike and Ride. Park the vehicle at the end, ride the bicycle to the origin, hike back to the vehicle, then drive back to the bicycle . Pretty involved but functional when all else fails. Map 4, Chapters 16 and 17.

There are no doubt other ways to take a hike, but you get the idea. Whichever way you choose, and where ever you go, be safe, take your camera, and enjoy the sights, smells, and acquaintances that you make along the trail.

Chapter 2

We Live In Hershey, PA and the Horse-Shoe Trail Runs Through It!
(HST Map 7, February 6, 1999.)

Yellow Blazes of the Horse-Shoe Trail are visible on my way to work and on my way home for about a mile on the Pennsylvania Route 322 corridor east of Hershey, PA. The HST turns to the south near the village of Campbelltown, traveling east, and turns north across the Milton Hershey School property, traveling west. I decided that this would be a good place to start hiking again after many years of two job work activity which did not leave time to play. A compelling factor initially was that I could leave from our home and return there at the end of the hike.

Diane agreed to drop me off where the HST crosses state Route 322 and to pick me up at the parking area for State Game Lands 145, on Route 117, after worship services.

Sunday, February 6, 1999, dawned with some clouds, a light breeze, and temperatures in the low 30's. A great day for a hike! I packed extra cold weather clothing, a cheese ball, some crackers, a bottle of water, tea bags, stove, fuel and other snacks into my old backpack and hoisted it into the vehicle.

At Route 322, I kissed Diane goodbye and told her I would call her on the cellular phone to arrange pick up after noon. Hoisting the back pack onto my shoulders brought back pleasant feelings and memories of past hikes, although the waist strap had to be relaxed about four inches to latch. I walked east along PA Route 322 to the Church of Nazarene and crossed their property to the adjacent field to see where the Horse Shoe Trail would lead me.

The trail followed a tree line south, along the edge of a field and through the driveway of a nice farm. Presently the blazes intersected and followed the edge of another field. I was pleasantly surprised that the trail was going through fields and farms with a very safe and nice view. The trail intersected Eby Road, which turned into Miller Road at the Lebanon/Dauphin County line. Much to my surprise the trail followed paved roads for the next several miles.

I had not examined the maps or guide in great detail before starting and was initially disappointed with this. As I walked east, on the road, there was no traffic and my concern diminished. When I came to the intersection of Locust Street and Eby Road, I had to cross a steady line of traffic to continue on the less traveled road.

Road crossings are dangerous, especially when there is no shoulder or berm. Traffic is an issue and a safety concern for walkers, backpackers, horsemen and bicyclists alike. The safety issues of the HST on public roads would become much more evident during my exploration of the HST and during many conversations with other hikers and horseback riders.

For all the concern, as I progressed away from the busy areas, the roads became much more enjoyable because I could hear vehicles approaching for several hundred yards and move from the road in a timely, and safe, manner. There is a lot of delay in standing on the side of the road and waiting for traffic to clear. In addition, this action severely breaks up the smooth rhythm of walking and interrupts whatever one was contemplating.

Reaching the plateau on Smith and Kreider Roads, I was inspired by the view. The small mountains north and east of Harrisburg, the terminus of the Horse Shoe Trail, were visible from this area. Also visible were the tops of the ridges at Manada Gap and Indiantown Gap, identified from the maps with the trail guide. A good view of Lebanon County was also observed with numerous fields, villages, and woodlands seen as though from an aircraft, but with the texture, sounds and smells of being there in person; up close and personal. This was a very pretty section of road and the view would not have been visible from inside the woodlands. In this area, the view was worth the risk of exposure to the one or two vehicles which passed me in this section, but there was no awesome view on most of the roads in the valley travelled to reach this area.

I regretted that I had not brought a camera along and compensated for this on later segments of the hike.

One of the nice things about starting close to home is that I could take photographs later without traveling long distances. The only major result of not bringing the camera is that the view, the sound, or the smell of the trail is never the same on different days. The view constantly changes with the season, weather, and hundreds of other variables.

A gentleman, working at his property, greeted me at the corner of Kreider Road, west of Lawn Road. I stopped and chatted for a few moments. This was my first encounter with a person along the trail. It was a friendly, informative and pleasant experience, the first of many more to come.

Continuing, I crossed Lawn Road and walked along a gravel driveway, past a picnic area where more people would probably greet hikers in warmer weather, and into the first wooded area of my route along the Horse-Shoe Trail. The woods were very limited. In a very short time, the trail came out to Drescher Road between numerous houses, but the road was wooded and the area pleasant.

Walking past Drescher Road, I observed the family home of a business acquaintance. I recognized the unique vehicle which often comes to our site to maintain equipment, then saw his name on the mail box. This family hosted trail users across the edge of their lawn rather than force them to take the road around - a safety and time benefit. I was very pleased but only later fully appreciated their thoughtfulness and courtesy. A reason for my personal good feelings was, in part, that by doing business with this person I was supporting good works in our community. Today, I benefitted from our relationship in a way which was never expected; I walked across their lawn on the Horse-Shoe Trail.

This observation strengthened my already positive impression of the man from this family I personally knew and I felt good about doing business with his employer.

The trail register box was located at the end of the meadow before the next wooded area. This box consisted of a nicely painted, waterproof, metal ammunition can mounted to a pole beside the trail. The trail register records hikers, trail maintenance and other information along the trail. I opened the can expecting to find a notebook and pen. The can was empty! Surprise! Perhaps the trail was closed for the season? I left a business card and put the date on the back.

Walking through the woods again, the trail narrowed to a single lane path. About four tenths of a mile later, the HST widened into a narrow street. Some litter was present at the edge of the woods where the street began and was deposited in cans which were along this road. Whether the cans were for this purpose is doubtful, but they presented what seemed at the time to be a fortuitous opportunity to deposit a rather large collection of litter into an appropriate receptacle. In any event, no one complained.

Route 117 was the next road crossing on the trail. This route was familiar and I had traveled it many times to company picnics, to reach a local golf course, and in general travel by vehicle. I never noticed the Horse-Shoe Trail crossing in the past and was fascinated that this trail had been here for the 20 years or so that I have been a resident of this area and had gone undetected.

Yellow blazes led me up Weber Avenue and into another woods on a wide dirt road. The road soon narrows into a dirt path. The next mile or so of the trail has been severely rutted by off road vehicles. Observing that the trail changes from two lane roads, to a dirt path less than three feet wide, to wide single lane roads, to streets, to paths across lawns, and repeats this pattern in an unpredictable sequence, I wondered where the Horse-Shoe Trail would lead next.

Soon, the question was answered. A gas line. Stepping into a clearing, a straight swath had been cut between the trees from ridge to ridge. How long did this take to accomplish? I wondered. Was this performed with heavy equipment in recent years, or with picks, shovels and axes in much earlier times? In any event, this swath through the woods facilitated the transmission of natural gas to the numerous homes in this area and further east. This swath represents one of the factors in a more productive society where we do not have to cut fire wood to heat our homes and cook our meals. Now we simply adjust the thermostat or light the burner. Of course, since we are now more productive, we send a check to the gas company each month for this convenience and hopefully earn more at other pursuits than cutting firewood.

Without natural gas, oil, electricity and other fuels, the entire north american continent would probably be hard pressed to provide enough trees for heat and cooking for our current population. Imagine the air quality if heating, cooking, transportation and industry still used firewood!

Unloved as it is, the swath through the woods and the transportation of mass energy supplies which it represents are better than most of the other possibilities I could imagine.

Passing a cottage and crossing the gas line again, the Horse-Shoe Trail enters woodland areas. The area has been logged, but the new growth trees provide a canopy and a fresh woodland environment. Walking here, I observed another phenomenon of the Horse-Shoe Trail, and other trails. When the trail is on level ground, gently rolling ground, or roads, there is very little erosion or sinking of the trail. Where the trail has a significant vertical rise in a relatively straight line, there is more erosion and the trail is sunken below the surface by as much as three or four feet! This condition was observed on the Appalachian Trail, near the terminus of the Horse-Shoe Trail, in the past and was attributed to local soil and drainage conditions. As I continued my journey and observed numerous other incidents of this phenomenon, my understanding would improve. The need for some basic engineering standards to be adopted for trail construction would be learned. These standards must be increased for specific trail uses. Foot trails require a minimal standard. Other uses need better trails.

Approaching the water tank at mile 13.5 on HST map 6, Lebanon County, numerous discarded water bottles and food wrappers were observed on the ground along the trail. I gathered the litter, taking what I could carry along. Litter which I could not carry was staged - collected and piled along the side of the trail - for later removal. This area of the trail was highly littered, and was the most heavily littered area, on the entire length of the Horse-Shoe Trail. This was also the first observation of another phenomenon: Litter is most frequent at the proximity to road crossings or access points. I later noted, with considerable appreciation for trail users, that over the entire 139.9 miles - per the trail guide - of the Horse-Shoe Trail, only two obvious pieces of litter were found more than one mile from road access points. This was amazing! I commend all who use the trail for this nice condition and urge new users to adopt the discipline which this condition manifests.

Based on the above observation, if you hike a section of trail that includes road crossings, or ends at a road crossing, bring a bag for collecting some litter and disposing of it properly. This will will not be a futile effort. There are waste receptacles near some trail access points. If a receptacle is not available for the waste you collect or pack out, please take it with you!

Continuing the walk toward the second crossing of Route 117 at state game lands 145, I enjoyed the view of a pretty lake to the east and looked at the foot prints of other walkers in the soft soil. Several sets of tracks were visible and all appeared to be from boots. It was probably the time of year.

Reaching the pick up point at the state game lands, I called home on the cellular phone. This is a luxury that comes at the expense of all of those telephone towers above the landscape, but is a most convenient technology at the current time. "Hi Honey, would you mind coming to bring me home?"

"I'll pick up Mom and come right away."

I removed my backpack, sat on the parking lot curb and brewed a cup of tea on the antique Tay Kit camp stove from my backpack. There is nothing like having cheese, crackers and a hot cup of tea in an outdoor restaurant on a cold day, knowing that your ride is on the way! It was a nice hike and I learned that I could still walk. So ended day one on the Horse-Shoe Trail.

Chapter
3

Still Close to Home.
(HST Map 7, February 14, 1999.)

February 14, Valentine's Day, 1999, was a little colder than a week earlier and the wind was brisk at about 20 to 25 miles per hour. The plan for the day was to stay close to home and explore the Horse Shoe Trail from Route 322 to the Hershey Cemetery, then call my Valentine via cellular phone for a ride home when I had reached this point. Because of wind chill, I had packed a moderate pair of gloves, a vapor barrier vest, a wool tassel cap and a wind breaker jacket with hood in addition to the stove, some tea, snacks and water, etc.

Wanting to get an early start, I checked the trail guide and maps for the area. Immediately I noticed that there are several thousand of the little squares, which indicate houses, missing from the map. Our house was built almost twenty years ago and it wasn't on the map? I checked the date: "1974" was the date on the map!

After careful examination of the map and mental addition of several major developments and numerous streets, I plotted a course from the house, through the maze of developments, across the Milton Hershey School grounds, and to the Horse-Shoe Trail. I checked the weather conditions. The air was brisk but the wind was not a factor around the house. I chose a sweater, cap and light gloves, kissed my Valentine, donned my pack and departed, through our neighborhood, to the Horse-Shoe Trail, about two miles distant.

Walking through our neighborhood and subsequent developments in Derry Township, I was pleased with the condition of the area. The residents and businesses maintain the properties and the community well.

Leaving the developments for the open field southwest of state Route 743, the wind became a factor. The trees and homes of the developments provided more shelter than I had anticipated and I soon became cold without their protection from the wind. I put on the vest and the wool cap and felt much better. Walking the driveway across the grounds of the Milton Hershey School I turned and walked backwards from time to time to thaw the windward ear. In the open spaces the wind was brutal. This was the one time I could remember where the ventilation between the backpack and my back was more than adequate. I was grateful for the backpack as a wind break.

Reaching the east side of the Milton Hershey School, I soon found the Horse Shoe Trail and turned northwest across the driveway and farm lanes that cross the fields. This was a large field for this area, almost a mile wide. The trail turned west along a driveway to some of the residences of the Milton Hershey School, then north again. Yellow blazes marking the route of the Horse-Shoe Trail were on the gate posts and on some of the larger rocks in the farm lane, as there was nothing else to paint!

Having a map and being familiar with the area was some comfort but as I followed the farm lane I became less and less confident that I was still on the trail. Aha! At last, a blaze was on a brick in the lane. A hundred steps later and the doubt returned. This became a cycle which would become routine. Often the next blaze was found within a hundred yards, sometimes they were not.

The lane passed close to a house near the village of Palmdale. A large dog came to greet me in a very assertive manner. I saw the yellow blazes on the trees to the right of the lane and moved in that direction. The dog kept a distance but barked constantly as I maintained my pace. The trail moved below the ridge line and was sheltered from the wind. I was grateful for the abatement of the wind but could do without the dog.

A man was at one of the out buildings smoking a cigar. He called to the dog and it went to his side and was quiet. "Thank you." I called rather loudly to overcome the wind.

"He won't bother you," the man said, walking toward me. "The problem with this dog is other dogs that aren't on a leash. This one is well trained to stay on the property, but some walkers come through with loose dogs and they chase the animals and fight with this one when he tries to chase them off," he said patting the dog's head. He told me that some users of Palmdale Park let their dogs stray all over the area chasing livestock. I learned that farmers appreciate guest dogs being controlled when they are visiting for various reasons.

We discussed a recent incident, which I had read about, where a pack of dogs attacked some fenced farm animals on an adjacent property and two "pet dogs" were destroyed by the farm's caretaker while attacking livestock which had been downed by the pack of dogs. The dogs' owners were in the local papers grieving for their pets which had been destroyed and threatening legal actions against the farmer. The farmer's question was: "If these dogs were pets, then why were they in these pens attacking our livestock?" It was a sad and emotionally charged situation all around.

Three areas of agreement were reached. First, if the dogs were pets, the owners should be reprimanded for letting their "pets" roam almost two miles from home. Second, the outcome of legal actions filed in this situation will defy all rational expectations of common mortals. Third, if the dogs were at home, under control, or on a leash, the problem would not have happened at all. This, last, has general merit. Please remember this tragedy if you bring your dog(s) on your walks or rides. Many property owners let the Horse-Shoe Trail, and other trails, cross their land as a courtesy. Please be respectful of this and help avoid unnecessary conflict between property owners and trail users over damages from, or to, uncontrolled dogs.

Having resolved the matter of the dogs attacking the livestock between us and agreeing that it would not be this simple in real life, I thanked the man for letting the trail cross his property and agreed to relay his request to other users of the trail that dogs be kept on a leash when they pass through the farm he tends. I followed the blazes to the village of Palmdale, then along the streets, described in the trail guide, to the golf course at the Hershey Country Club.

Walking into Palmdale, I realized that I had achieved a milestone: I had completed Map 7 of the Horse-Shoe Trail! While this is only 8 miles, there are only 9 maps. From the perspective of completing one ninth of the maps, this was a major achievement. From the perspective of 8 miles of 139.9 miles, it was no big deal. I kept the one ninth perspective in mind as I searched for a blaze to tell me where to turn east toward Lingle Road. I never found this blaze!

After searching for yellow blazes on trees, rocks and in the dirt, I followed the railroad tracks east to the bridge which carries Lingle Road over the tracks. I climbed up to the road. Aha! A yellow blaze was on a telephone pole. I turned around and followed the blazes south to see where the Horse-Shoe Trail came out from the golf course. The trail is on the gravel road which goes through the field, west, to the golf course. Amazing!

Continuing north along Lingle Road, the trail turns left along a quarry. As I reached this turn, several eastern blue birds crossed the road in front me from trees on my left into the woods to the right. The birds checked each branch they landed on for something to eat, then moved along. They were a pretty sight. With the drab colors of winter still dominating the land, the brilliant blue and yellow plumage of these bludbirds provided a preview of the coming spring.

Entering the fenced area along the quarry another session of "seek the yellow blazes" was engaged. Vines quickly cover blazes on trees and it is difficult to maintain a walking pace when the vines are so thick that their stems completely cover the blazes on the trees. Eventually I found some blazes on poles, rocks, and stumps which led me through this section but not without some searching and frustration.

A stone structure at the end of the quarry was interesting from a historical perspective. I have no idea of the purpose of this specific structure however, it is an example of the use of stone in buildings where the actual method of placing stones during construction can be observed. There were also some artifacts from old railroad activity. Whether this railroad was specific to the quarry operation or part of a more generic railroad, I do not know. The underbrush and downed trees were so thick that I had a very difficult time picking my way through this area, even when I could see the yellow blazes. Eventually I got through and walked on a very nice farm road to PA Route 743. The lane was closed from Route 743 by a gate.

I walked up to the Hershey Cemetery. Here, the view of Hershey was outstanding although the wind was bone chilling. I put on my hooded jacket and removed the cellular phone from the backpack. "Hi Honey, can you come and get me?"

"I'll be there in a few minutes."

This was great! I liked the convenience of the cellular phone. I liked that I could go for a hike across a field, a school campus, over hill and dale, down streets of a village, past golf courses, old railroads, quarries, and examine these interesting sights at my leisure. The presence of blue birds, and other wildlife, added a pleasant dimension.

Being close to home was also a good feeling. The fact that I had spent an enjoyable time exploring new and fascinating areas in the community we had lived in for the past twenty years impressed me. There is so much history off the road that I had never seen before but which I had driven vehicles past hundreds of times, that I was very surprised. The best part is that all of these interesting things are only a few miles from home!

Speaking with the man near Palmdale was interesting. The views were outstanding. I had been lost, sought blazes and found my way. One entire map of the nine in the guide book had been completed today.

It was a great hike!

So ended day two on the Horse-Shoe Trail.

Chapter
4

Road Walking
(HST Map 8, February 19 & 20, 1999.)

Planning access to and return from the Horse-Shoe Trail hikes became more involved as the distance from home increased. The ease of starting from home and calling on the cellular phone for a ride, which would take just a few moments, became more demanding on my bride with increasing distance from home, requiring better coordination and scheduling. As the locations to be hiked were further away, the ride, almost an hour to complete, was now, an item which should be scheduled in advance.

For the weekend of February 19 and 20, 1999, I wanted to complete Map 8 of the Horse-Shoe Trail, of which about twelve miles remained. We decided to leave one vehicle at PA Route 22 and drop me off at Manada Gap. This would give me a distance of about five miles on the first day, February 19th. If everything worked out well, I could be dropped off at PA Route 22 and walk home from there on the 20th. We drove out during the week to scout the drop off point and to look for a parking place for my vehicle. I mistakenly thought the Horse-Shoe Trail crossed PA Route 443 because my map showed this to be so. After driving back and forth several times, we followed the HST blazes along Cliff Road to Furnace Road and picked a drop off point near Manada Creek, on Furnace Road. Parking along PA Route 22 was very good.

On the morning of February 19, 1999, I parked my vehicle at PA Route 22 and Diane dropped me off on Furnace Road. I walked along Furnace Road to Ridge Road to Manada Bottom Road to Jonestown Road to North Mill Road and came to the vehicle. Although these were relatively rural roads there was some traffic and woods for calls of nature. The roads had no shoulders and it was a challenge to get out of the way for traffic on occasion. Be especially careful crossing under Interstate 81.

There were no people out of doors except in vehicles. In many areas, where there were pull offs from the road, litter and household garbage had been dumped on the ground and in the springs and small streams prevalent in the area. It was almost as though these pull offs were a new design of dumpster for rural areas and people were faithfully using them for disposal of unwanted furniture, appliances, tires and other trash.

These dump sites are a common observation along rural roads in this part of Dauphin County and it is sad because this is the watershed for much of Lebanon and Dauphin County's drinking water. There was little or no litter on the actual Horse-Shoe Trail. More litter and garbage was seen dumped along roads in this area and to the north, in Dauphin County, than on any other area on this hike; and all of it was immediately adjacent roads. Not a happy thought.

I reached the vehicle at PA Route 22. I was disappointed with the dumping and with walking on paved roads the entire distance. Isn't there someone who enforces dumping regulations or cleans up in Dauphin County? People are dumping garbage in our drinking water! It was not a happy hike! The Horse-Shoe Trail also needs help here.

So ended day three on the Horse-Shoe Trail.

On February 20 Diane dropped me off at PA Route 22. I planned to walk home. There were houses on both sides of S. Mill Road, Carlson Road and Crawford Road which were not on the map. It was a long time since I had last used this relic, the map was 25 years old! The maps in the trail guide are also historic documents. In addition to the new houses, there are entire new streets and roads.

Do you remember the bathroom? You know, the one which used to be behind the second tree on the left? Well, the tree is now a street and the bathroom has been replaced with a housing development! The dirt path through the woods is now a paved road. If you are going to walk this section, take care of your basic functions while a vehicle is available because the next tree on the left, or right, is about five miles away. The truck stops on Route 39 are much closer.

The Horse-Shoe Trail follows Crooked Hill Road, Sand Beach Road, Early Mill Road, Trail Road, and East Canal Street. Just when I was wondering which road or street I would walk next, the trail turned left into a meadow along a dirt path. Oh look, a tree! I was delighted to be off the roads and followed the trail along the dirt path where it descends toward Swatara Creek.

Posted beside the trail was a plaque. It read: *"This sign marks the beginning of eight miles of THE HORSE-SHOE TRAIL on Milton Hershey School property restored in 1992 as an Eagle Scout Project by Michael L. Barbu '93 of the schools Explorer Post 475. It is maintained by the Explorers of Post 475"*

I was impressed that the Horse-Shoe Trail still runs across eight miles of Milton Hershey School property. I reflected that this project probably has provided a benefit to many hundreds of people who have used this trail, including myself. It was nice of Mr. Barbu and his Scout leaders to undertake this community service and leadership project, and it is nice of the Milton Hershey School to continue to make the use of the land available to hikers and riders who pass through.

After descending, the trail crosses bottom lands along the Swatara Creek, then follows the creek west to cross a bridge on Sand Hill Road. Remnants of the Union Canal system are still present. I returned and photographed this area from the bridge over the Swatara Creek during September, 1999. The leaves had started to change. *(See Photographs 1 and 2)*

South of the Swatara Creek, the trail passes a residence house of the Milton Hershey School then ascends a relatively steep hill. The view from this hill is awe inspiring, especially after walking about ten miles of paved roads in the last two days without a break. *(See Photographs 3 and 4)*

Boat House Park, operated by Derry Township Parks and Recreation, is just to the west of where Sand Beach Road crosses the Swatara Creek. There is ample parking here and this is within a mile of the summit of the hill with the awe inspiring view. If you need some inspiration and only have an hour or so, park at the park, follow the yellow blazes to the south, and check out the view from this hill.

Leaving the view to the north, east and west, I followed the trail south and continued toward home. About 30 deer were milling about in the woods and most just stared at me as I passed. The trail crossed Peffley Road and went down a driveway of one property, then crossed the paved road and coursed between a house and the garage of the next property. Although I did not understand the significance of this generosity at the time, I came to have an appreciation for the people who were so generous as to let hikers and horsemen alike travel across their lawns, lanes, forests and fields. In many cases, such as this, the trail passed within several feet of occupied buildings. What a dichotomy between walking on the road and walking beside someone's garage, through their yard! I returned in September and photographed this site as an example of community spirit! *(See Photograph 5 and look closely at the left edge of the shed to see the blaze on the left edge of the white building, which marks the Horse-Shoe Trail.)*

At the end of the yard, the trail skirts a nice pine grove. This was a very pleasant area. Leaving the pines, I walked along another road to Hershey Cemetery and set a route for home. I was so grateful to walk on trails rather than roads for the last several miles that I committed myself to write a letter to the management at Milton Hershey School to express my appreciation for their hospitality, which I did.

Walking along PA Route 743 into the town of Hershey, I was pleased with this town. It is neat, clean, and smells like someone is baking chocolate brownies. I could see the activities at Hershey Park. Although crossing the railroad bridge from Hershey Park Drive to the Hershey Country Club was probably one of the most challenging feats of the day, the sidewalks and walking trails took me home without any further exposure to parallel traffic.

I walked past the Hershey Foods offices, across the high school property, past the public library and up the walking trail to our home, reflecting how great it is to have a trail for the citizens to walk or bicycle to the schools and library in Derry Township. This trail is even wheel chair friendly!

After the road walking, it was a great hike! It was also great to be home. During this segment of the trail I better understoof the need to plan for open space for walking trails, bicycle trails, horse trails or for playing games. Otherwise we will be arguing about why state game lands should accommodate vehicles rather than being set aside for hunting, and why basketball courts should be installed on highways.

It was also observed that Dauphin County needs to organize an effort to clean up the trash from their watershed areas.

So ended day four on the Horse-Shoe Trail.

Chapter
5

White Out on the Horse-Shoe Trail
(HST Map 9, March 6, 1999.)

"CAUTION: From here on the area is remote, do not travel alone, carry food and water. During hunting season wear brightly colored clothing." The trail guide admonished. The next section was through forests and clearings at the tops of the high hills, which further south are called "balds." The Appalachian Trail (AT) access route to the Horse-Shoe Trail was through this area of mixed forest which is unbroken for more than 25 miles, to the east, from the Susquehanna River.

Knowing this was a remote area, and planning to hike alone, my backpack contained stove, fuel, water proof clothing, extra gloves, first aid supplies, food and snacks for three or four days. Also, a tarp for emergency shelter. There was no tent or sleeping bag. I had the cellular phone, that convenient device to stay in touch with the rest of the world, and a spare battery pack for the cellular phone.

The plan for today was to take one vehicle, travel to the intersection of PA Route 325 and the Appalachian Trail, park the vehicle, then hike the AT to the terminus of the Horse-Shoe Trail. From there, to hike southwest on the HST to the pick up point in Stony Creek Valley, a distance of about 12 miles. I looked forward to completing this section since, when completed, the remaining distance on the HST in Dauphin County could be accomplished in one day's walk.

Walking 7 or 8 miles per day, one or two days per week, Dauphin County's 35.2 miles of Horse-Shoe Trail seemed to go on forever! I was ready to try for more distance.

Diane and I scouted the pick up point the week before. Yes, it was on a narrow dirt back road. Yes, it was a 40 mile round trip, or more, from home for each vehicle. And most importantly, yes, the Horse-Shoe Trail was accessible from the dirt road east of Dauphin, PA before the road gate which closes the game lands to vehicle traffic on the converted railroad bed. The area is closed to vehicles but stays open to bicycles and walkers most of the year, which is nice. One week each year, the gates are opened to one way vehicle traffic so that drivers and those who otherwise cannot access the forests, can see the splendor of the autumn leaves in the hardwood forests which extend for about 26 miles to Goldmine Road. The local newspapers advertise the dates.

This road is very nice to travel on foot, horse or bicycle most of the year, but avoid the traffic in the area on the one week the railroad trail is open to vehicles.

Diane's schedule was to work in the morning. She would then be able to pick me up in the afternoon. "I'll call you on the cellular phone from the ridge above Stony Valley," I promised, then drove to the trail head for the Appalachian Trail.

Parking at the trail head it was obvious that someone considered this area one of the numerous local "Dauphin Dumpsters" since there were mattresses, box springs and garbage dumped in the parking area. This area of Dauphin County, PA, where roads have pull offs or parking areas, so often have trash stacked on them that it reminds me of Detroit slums on garbage day, without the row houses!

The temperature was in the high twenties or low thirties as I put on the backpack, crossed Clark's Creek, and started across bottom lands on the Appalachian Trail. The sky was clear to the west and there was a heavy line of cloud cover to the east northeast. Since the prevailing winds are from the west, I anticipated a beautiful day for hiking; surely the clouds were moving away and the sky will clear I thought at the time.

Passing Clark's Creek, to the left of the AT traveling east, I saw a submerged tree in the clear water of the creek and looked for fish in the shadow. There were none visible. This tree would be a real hazard for a canoe. It would not be visible to canoes traveling on the surface of the water except for the exposed roots protruding on the bank from where the tree had fallen.

The AT followed an access road south for a short distance on level ground, crossed the water pipeline to the City of Harrisburg from the De Hart Dam, about a mile or so upstream, then turned east and started to ascend to the summit of Sharp Mountain.

Criticism has often been leveled at those of us who call the ridges of the Appalachian Chain "Mountains," since the highest elevation is only slightly above 2,400 feet. The Appalachians are old mountains which have worn down but still provide beautiful views and an uplifting experience. Those of us who grew up on their slumped shoulders and wooded sides, enjoy the views of sheltered valleys and fertile farms from the few remaining rock pinnacles. We love and appreciate these "Mountains." Please humor our use of the term.

The ascent of Sharps Mountain is between 800 and 1,000 feet over a distance of three miles or so. The elevations indicated on the map with the trail guide are printed so small I can't read them with, or without, my glasses. It is not a vertical rise, but a fair slope which goes on for a considerable distance through forests and fields of boulders.

Foot placement requires close attention on the lower slopes of this ascent. The AT has been badly eroded in some areas and power equipment appears to have been used to cut a new corridor into the hillside. (Perhaps it was dirt bikes or a back hoe.) Where the new corridor is cut into the underlying stone and soil it forms a channel because the material removed to form the trail has been stacked on the down slope side of the trail. Storm water runs over the top of the cut on the side by the mountain into this channel. The water then follows the channel because the trail is lower than the side of the cut away from the mountain.

Every 100 feet or so there is a trench to move the water from the channel over the downstream hillside. During periods of water flow, the trail's channel transforms the gentle flow of storm water from a shallow sheet of water, perhaps 1/16 inch deep by a hundred feet wide; into a channeled flow of water, perhaps seven inches deep by one foot wide, which is contained in the channel. Water that would naturally flow, gently and slowly, across the trail in very shallow sheets is now directed onto the trail in volume. Gravity and the slope of the trail combine to transform this channeled water into a formidable force which rushes down the trail with phenomenal kinetic energy, removing virtually everything in its path. Grass, small stones, and soil have been scoured away by the force of this channeled water. Numerous trees have been toppled by removal of the supporting soils from their roots and lay across the trail. Was this section intentionally designed so that each rainfall would remove the trail surface and keep the trail route challenging? I think not!

A hydraulic mining machine, in essence, excavates the trail in this area with each rain storm or snow melt. At the areas where there is a steep slope, the AT has been effectively excavated by storm water. Standing on the remaining rocks, I could not see over the down slope edge of the trench from the erosion gully which is the new AT.

If you do trail maintenance, please consult with an engineer; such as at the Department of Transportation, the local National Guard Engineering Battalion, the Civil Engineering Department at the local University, on the internet, or where someone is available who has designed or built a functional storm water control system. They can help locate a resource to identify proper slopes, drains and grades before your team constructs another "hydraulic mining machine".

On the other hand, if you removed the water retarding steps to make the trail easier to ride over, shame on you! This action has caused a lot of damage.

The challenge was irresistible. I parked the pack and removed my orange vest. An hour or so was spent placing stones into the trenches and constructing diverting dams to move the water pathway from long stretches of channeled trail into a sheet flow over the down slope side of the trail in this area. Don't despair! The trail still needs your help. Please bring a loose rock from the direction you are traveling from and drop it into one of the trenches in this area. Don't fall in! You may need climbing gear to get out.

Darkness covered the land. I looked up in surprise. Clouds which I earlier believed had left, were back. A heavy, dark, mass of clouds with a straight leading edge had covered the sun. Sleet began falling. The expectation and hope of a clear sky was gone. The wet weather qualities of my new hiking clothing would be tested for the first time.

Precipitation brought change on the trail. The dry rock was now glistening with moisture and a mist, almost a light fog, was forming just above the surface of the forest floor. I continued up the trail and was fascinated as the mist turned into an ankle deep fog as I walked. About half way to the terminus of the Horse-Shoe Trail a mine shaft has been dug into the side of the mountain. The opening is closed but brightly colored orange material is below the water which seeps from the mine and has discolored the side of the mountain in this area. Perhaps this has something to do with the absence of fish in Clark's Creek below?

The acid seeping from the side of the mountain has discolored the mined materials which have been dumped in a fan shaped pile on the down hill side of the mountain. It looked like a partially scabbed knife wound. The first aid kit I carried was comprehensive but could not close this wound! I felt helpless. Continuing on, I felt as if I were abandoning an injured friend in desperate need.

I would try to get help: Help! Is anyone out there who would like to treat a serious environmental wound? Sharps Mountain is bleeding to death! A mine shaft has penetrated its heart! Send a remedial team to north latitude 40 degrees, 26 minutes and 45 seconds by west longitude 76 degrees, 45 minutes and no seconds. Watch for DeHart Dam just to the north and insert the team at the clearing with the orange/yellow stain on a true heading of 181 degrees from the north west corner of De Hart Dam at a distance of about 2,100 meters. Bring several hundred tons of high calcium limestone to treat the acid, and a 10 foot section of 12 inch diameter plastic pipe to carry the mine drainage under the trail.

Snow was now falling steadily. It had covered the trail and the forest floor. Fog was covering the bottoms of the trees, to about a foot deep. The rough, loose, rock surface of the trail turned into a wide smooth trail which, according to the Appalachian Trail Guide, was once a stagecoach trail. This was an impressive man made feature since it has been in place for more than a hundred and fifty years and is still not rutted or eroded. I made a note for when I work on a trail to install similar slopes, stone drainage systems, and surfacing systems to those found here so that the work will last for the next hundred years or so. This stagecoach trail should be recorded as a national civil engineering accomplishment.

The toes of my boots were now flipping off clumps of snow as I walked and the sounds of the wind overhead were those of a major storm, shrieking and howling above the sheltering ridge of the mountain. The snow was falling so densely now that the sky was no longer visible and the entire forest was taking on a blanket of white. Fog climbed higher into the air. The world around me was changing from early spring to a winter landscape, blanketed with fog.

Near the Horse-Shoe Trail the snow was five to six inches deep. The AT was protected from the fury of the storm, which was blowing branches from the trees on the top of the ridge. The clouds had moved over the area from the northeast but the surface winds were from the southwest.

The terminus of the Horse-Shoe Trail was just in front of me. The wind was blowing so forcefully through the gap where the HST and AT meet, that the snow was falling horizontally and was being whipped into the trees and forest floor at about 60 mph. Loose tree branches were also falling in the exposed area. I recognized the hazard this presented and braced myself against the force of the wind beyond the sheltered area. Pushed backward at first by the force of the wind, I struggled to walk to where the trail dropped below the ridge. The snow and blowing fog were so dense here that visibility was down to about ten feet or less. The snow was being blown so forcefully that it coated my glasses about 1/4 inch thick when I raised my face to look for the trail register. I wiped my glasses and kept the visor of my hat pointed down. Even with clear glasses visibility was almost zero due to fog and snow. I could feel my body temperature dropping perceptibly, almost with each step. This could be very dangerous!

There was no change in wind speed or improvement in visibility as I reached the trail register box about 30 yards from the sheltered section of the AT. I started shaking with a chill and immediately retreated to the sheltered area behind the ridge to put on more and warmer clothing. With a sigh of relief from the bitter wind chill, and for the comfort of the sheltered area, I removed the backpack and vest, shaking the wet snow from the vest and other clothing. I had a spiral bound notebook in the backpack, which I also removed.

Standing in this sheltered area, hearing tree branches falling near by, I could understand one purpose some of the "mysterious"stone shelters constructed in the north eastern United States would have served. These structures may have been constructed to protect early woodland inhabitants from the hazards of falling trees, and temperatures, during high winds.

Vapor barrier shirt and water repellent trousers were pulled on as I contemplated the function of some of the stone shelters I had seen in areas further north. Water repellent clothing was pulled on over my damp gear. Again, I attempted to walk the top of the ridge. Stepping into the driving snow, benefits of the rain clothing were obvious. My body temperature was fine. Reaching the top of the ridge, I opened the register box and the register was actually there! The last trail register box had been empty.

I removed a heavy glove to write in the register and the exposed hand immediately became cold. As I wrote the date, a brilliant flash of lightning and the deafening roar of thunder caused me to leap away from the tree, a fright reflex?

The trial log and pen were dropped into the snow.

Sounds from a tree falling to the ground somewhere close to the right of the trail was heard above the wind but could not be seen. I removed my glasses and there was no change in visibility. It was a white out!

Cleaning off the trail register and finding the pen took only a few moments. During this time my exposed hand had become numb from the wind chill. I shook the snow from my glove then put it back on. I wrote a brief entry in the trail log then returned the log book and the pen to the metal box with shaking hands.

I wanted to continue my walk. What consequences would result? I considered this. The trail from here was unknown, visibility was zero, and trees were being blown over by the wind, or being shattered by lightning. Risks of continuing were real and there was a serious potential of exposure, injury, or worse. Letting reason prevail, and avoiding the potential embarrassment of having to be rescued after a bad fall or whatever, I aborted the hike and turned back to the sheltered path of the AT, following my rapidly vanishing foot prints in the snow.

Sheltered again, I stopped in a clearing under a pine tree which had stopped the snow from reaching the ground. I took out the cellular phone to call Diane. There was no signal! The cellular phone was useless.

Being in the very clouds the snow was falling from was a unique experience. I took photographs of the white out on the Horse-Shoe Trail and of the AT, from this area. The photographs of the white out on the HST did not take; those in the sheltered area of the AT did. *(Photograph 6).*

Descending carefully, the conditions improved with diminished altitude and the walk along the bottom lands was not much different than the walk up. I did notice that it was very wet now and congratulated myself on the wisdom of my choice.

Returning to the vehicle and heaving a sigh of relief, I removed the backpack, changed into dry clothing and drove home.

Today I learned that very bad conditions could be encountered in a friendly and familiar area. I also learned that use of proper clothing makes a great difference in personal comfort during a nasty storm, and that the cellular phone has a severe limitation – when you need it the absolute most, it may not function due to lack of signal or whatever.

A mystery had been solved. I now understood why stone trench shelters had been constructed in the deep woods to the north. Stone was available, it was in usable sizes, and it provided very good protection from falling branches or entire trees. Seeing where trees had been blown down like tall grass is one thing. Actually being under them during a major storm and without a strong shelter is quite a different experience!

So ended day 5 on the Horse-Shoe Trail. It was a great hike!

Chapter
6

Use at Your Own Risk!
(HST Map 9, March 13, 1999.)

Snow capped the ridges of the mountains visible near my home on Friday. The plan for Saturday was to hike a shorter route to compensate for the snow but still to work toward completing the Dauphin County segment of the Horse-Shoe Trail. I settled on the section from Stony Creek, the parking point for the start, to Sleepy Hollow Road, the pick up point for the second vehicle. There was cellular phone service in this area. I had checked!

Parking the vehicle in Stony Valley, at one of the tight spaces along the narrow dirt road, I was very pleased that there was no garbage dumped here.

Following the dirt road on the abandoned railroad bed, the point where the Horse-Shoe Trail turned south into the forest was soon reached. There was snow in the wooded areas. The snow was only an inch or so deep at this point. I stopped to review the trail guide.

"Cross Stony Creek. Ford or use cable bridge at your own risk. (Swimming hole upstream)," the trail guide read. I envisioned a cable suspension bridge, with a plank deck, spanning Stony Creek. Pocketing the trail guide, I followed the yellow blazes into the woods. The pleasant sound of water rather gently tumbling over rocks, below, became more audible, but never actually loud, with my approach.

Reaching the creek bank I looked for the bridge. There was no bridge! Had the winter storms washed it out? Did it collapse of its own weight? It had vanished.

Wait! What's on the side of the large fir tree? A ladder? Yes! There were three cables spanning the creek about ten feet above the water. The three cables were one above the other, similar to the power lines which enter a home but much further apart. The cables ended in large fir trees on each side of the creek. Wooden ladders had been fixed to the sides of the trees to access the cables. Very interesting indeed. How do you cross this, hand over hand?

I had crossed single rope bridges before. Many years before! The technique is to stand beside a waist high rope which is stretched tightly between anchor points on each side of the obstacle to be crossed. Lay face down on the rope, keeping the rope centered under your body. Then place the leg adjacent the rope on top of the rope, pulling this leg up toward the center of your body such that the top of your toes (in the boot, if worn) rests on the top of the rope. The foot on the ground acts as a stabilizing support until you make enough forward progress to clear the ground. With the hands in front and the back of your toes (top of one boot) on the rope, propulsion is provided by pulling with the hands and pushing with the foot over the rope – gently. The leg away from the rope hangs down for ballast during crossing. If you fall from the rope, you can resort to hand over hand. The purpose of this rope crossing technique was that when anyone failed in their crossing, for whatever reason, the next person had a clear rope for their attempt at a crossing! This had worked very well under different conditions but I didn't have a good feeling about using this technique here.

Another Technique used in the past for crossing a single cable was to use a pulley fastened to a climbing or parachute harness. The cable was installed from a high point on the departure side to a lower point on the receiving side. For a return trip, there needed to be another cable anchored in the opposite fashion since gravity propelled the passenger. This was a very efficient type of crossing. The pulley was locked onto the cable, clipped to the harness, and the crossing was one step away. Similarly, a short length of rope could be used as the pulley and handle by looping this over the cable and hanging onto the ends during the crossing, depending on the users and their physical condition. Needed were smooth sloped cables, rope and a harness. I had none of these.

Deciding to cross by placing my feet on the lower cable, my hands on the upper cable, and wishing I had a carabineer or some other means to secure the backpack to the cables, I climbed the ladder and stepped gingerly onto the cable bridge. Close to the tree, the cables were fairly tight. I examined the view of Stony Creek. It was a beautiful sight from here.

Working my way toward the center of the cables, it became obvious that the cable bearing my weight, the bottom one, was sagging much more than the top one. Also, there was much more sag in the middle than at the edges. The cables twisted! My feet were pointing down stream and my head was pointing upstream. I hung on desperately, face up. I was looking up at the bottom branches of the fir trees from my now horizontal position about ten feet above the cold water. The center cable was under my chin. This cable slipped over my chin and jammed my lips, nose, glasses and hat up my face. The cable then swung back and rapped me on top of the head with a dull thunk and a lot of pain. Ouch! My eyes watered and I almost fell. The center cable settled behind my head and rested on the backpack frame.

Cold water, gurgling over the rocks below could be heard but not seen. Trembling, I and continued across, moving each hand and foot about five or six inches at a time. The cables continued to shake and my hands began to cramp. Could I make this hand over hand with the backpack? I wasn't sure. I tried to use the center cable to take some of the weight from my arms but was concerned that it would snap back over my head and break my glasses, nose or teeth. I was afraid to take my feet from the bottom cable because I might fall or the center cable may be over the backpack pins. I could end up hanging from the harness in such a way that I could not reach the cables at all. This is not a good situation, I thought.

Tension on the cables increased as I approached the far side of the bridge and the cable anchors in the fir tree. With the increased tension came better orientation and balance. I managed to get my feet back under me and free the center cable from between my neck and the backpack without losing my glasses or breaking body parts. Shaking uncontrollably from the unaccustomed strain on my arms, I stepped onto the cable anchors and rested. Wow!

Gradually my pulse, adrenalin and shaking came under control. With a last appreciative look at the fine view of Stony Creek from the eye which could focus through a lens of my still dislocated glasses, I started to climb down from the cables. The ladder was on the other side of the cables from the ladder where I had started.

Uttering a silent oath I attempted to duck under the center cable without losing my still marginally secured glasses and hat. The cable kept hanging up on the backpack when I attempted to cross under it. Releasing the waist belt and loosening the shoulder harness, I slid the backpack down and managed to get under the cable and down the ladder without losing my glasses, hat or taking a polar bear plunge into Stony Creek.

I stopped on the bank, still somewhat shaken from the Cable Bridge. I now understood perfectly why the trail guide describing this crossing reads: "Use at your own risk!" (*Photographs 7 and 8)*

Chapter 7

"Did You Hear the Rabbit?"
(HST Map 9, March 13, 1999.)

With my new understanding of the need for a carabineer or other method to transport a backpack over a cable bridge, I took a long drink of water, checked out the view of the creek and cable bridge again, packed up and headed south through the pine forest in the bottom lands. This is a very beautiful section of trail and in a short time the Horse-Shoe Trail enters the pipeline right of way for the Buckeye Pipeline Company's fuel transmission pipeline.

Snow was about 3 or 4 inches deep at the clearing for the pipeline. The trail and pipeline followed a gradually increasing slope to the snow covered top of Second Mountain, visible about one and one half miles ahead, southeast, in a straight line from Stony Creek. Third Mountain, also snow covered, was visible about the same distance from Stony Creek to the northwest. I observed that the Buckeye pipeline connected the tops of both mountains and was cleared of brush and trees the entire way. This minor observation (Photograph 9) would become important on a later hike in the dark.

The effort of ascending Second Mountain with my overweight body and the additional thirty five pounds of pack soon created an appreciation for the cool weather. I opened the tabs, vents, and zippers of the vest, jacket and shirt. I continud to sweat profusely as I walked up the snow covered right of way.

Vehicle tracks were noted on the pipeline clearing about one quarter of a mile ahead. I wondered what vehicles were back here? A vertical pipe was noted at the location of the vehicle tracks and there appeared to be a dark object at the bottom of this pipe. Because of a slight depression in the slope, I could not see the base of the pipe or the object clearly.

A blue sleeping bag was noted in the woods to the left. The sleeping bag appeared empty and in worse condition than me. I thought of trail stories which told how people discarded extra equipment for the first several miles. I wondered whether this sleeping bag had been discarded in the same manner as I struggled to keep moving slowly up the mountain.

A small, red, moving object appeared in stark contrast to the snow at the top of Second Mountain. It was now about a mile away. It looked like a red tack moving across a wall of white wallpaper from across a very large room. Who or what was this and what were they doing in the middle of a game lands? Poachers? Not in a red outfit. Not on a Saturday. I was concerned because the area is normally closed to vehicles and it was the wrong time of year to be mowing grass!

Scanning the trail ahead and to the sides, I looked for rock formations and other places where I could be less obvious than the middle of the pipeline, contrasted against snow. I moved closer to the trees. In the depression, just ahead, there were several downed trees and a small drainage area where grass was showing. There were some large rocks beyond the grass without a snow field in front of them. I moved in that direction.

The red dot on top of Second Mountain developed a vehicle under it as it moved closer, about a quarter of a mile, then stopped. I could now see a person, who removed the red dot, apparently a helmet, and took something from the vehicle and placed it on the ground. Some time was spent at the site of the object on the ground by the person from the vehicle. The person again put on the red helmet and moved toward me.

I looked at the vertical pipe protruding up from the pipeline, which was now clearly visible from where I stood. There was an object on the ground at the base of this pipe. The object was olive drab in color and shaped like a piece of 6 inch x 6 inch lumber about 15 inches long. Wires ran from this box into the vertical pipe. What are the wires for? My initial thoughts were from watching too many movies which featured unnecessary and explosive special effects. Realistic thoughts were that perhaps a device had been installed to detect leakage from the pipeline?

The vehicle stopped again after traveling an additional one fourth mile or so. Again, the person dismounted and took a package to what may have been another vertical pipe. I walked back to the pipeline, convinced that the person was doing some sort of maintenance or characterization work on the actual pipeline.

Examining the box from a short distance, it appeared to be a sound or vibration monitoring system. I had seen very similiar equipment used on very large water treatment systems in the past. They could have been anything, but had too many wires for a more basic need. My concerns were now replaced with curiosity.

Walking at the edge of the pipeline, hoping not to disturb whatever was being monitored, I approached the next vertical pipe as the person in the red helmet was also moving toward it. The vehicle was a four wheel all terrain vehicle and handled the snow very well. The vehicle stopped at the vertical pipe and a man removed his helmet, took an olive drab box from the back of the four wheel drive all terrain vehicle and began to install it as I approached. "Are you going to the top of the hill?" He asked.

"Yes," I responded.

"Please walk lightly around where we have these monitors set up. There is an orange ribbon at each location. I would appreciate if you can avoid them as much as possible since the vibrations from walking close to them will set them off."

"What are you measuring?" I asked.

"We have a special rabbit which comes through the pipe. The package has transponders and a recorder which measures and record the sounds of the rabbit's passage. We analyze the data to determine the wall thickness of the pipe between the monitoring stations."

"That's pretty interesting."

"You can walk within about six feet or so of the boxes. Just go lightly, don't stomp your feet, and they will be fine."

Continuing up the slope, I avoided the other three devices and didn't stomp my feet. A monument of some sort was examined on the west side of the pipeline where the slope became more difficult. I photographed this object, but still have not determined what it is or what it marks.

Other hikers were visible coming from the southeast as I reached the top of the ridge and looked down the other side. Suddenly, a bicycle came out of the woods on a side trail and started down the mountain to the southeast. There was a sharp squeal as the bicyclist appeared to slow his descent and to avoid the other walkers. In the quiet of this area, the squeal was surprisingly loud, especially at 200 yards or so.

Enjoying the view from the summit, I opened the backpack and took out some snacks, water, the camera and the cellular phone. Yes, there was a signal! Relishing an apple, I spoke with the other hikers and took their photograph. I then prevailed on them to photograph me with my camera. (Photograph 10) I always liked to be on the top of mountains, hills, trees, or whatever. The view, as a reward for the climb, probably has something to do with this.

Utilizing that most convenient device, I called home. "Hi Honey, I'm at the top of the Second Mountain. The view of Harrisburg and the surrounding area is awesome."

"When do you want me to come for you?"

"Give me about an hour before you leave, then when you get here I will be beyond the Fishing Creek Elementary School and you can pick me up on Sleepy Hollow or East Appalachian Trail Road."

"OK. I'll see you in about two hours."

How convenient! I really appreciate the support of my wife and the convenience of the cellular phone. Only four ounces and it can call anywhere. Not like those old forty pound radios that could only call ten miles or so, even from an elevated point like this. Life is great. The apple was consumed, everything was bagged and packed and I started southeast and down the Horse-Shoe Trail. The four wheel all terrain vehicle and the driver crested the mountain with a crunching of snow and ice. The driver stopped beside me.

"Did you hear the rabbit?"

"I heard a squeal a short while ago but I thought it was the brakes on a bicycle," I replied. The volume of the noise was very loud for the distance of the bicycle at the time.

"That should have been the rabbit. It actually squeals when it comes through the pipe," the pipeline man explained.

"I knew they put a ball or something called a 'rabbit' between different products in the pipelines to keep them separate, but I never knew of one to squeal loud enough to hear it above the ground," I stated.

"This rabbit has a special collar to help measure the insides of the pipe. It may squeal loud enough that you can hear it. It should have passed under here about twenty minutes ago."

"That's when I heard the squeal, but I saw the bicycle and assumed it was from the brakes."

"I don't know. Have a good hike," he said and waved as he continued down the mountain.

Descending was much quicker than the climb to here. I wondered if I had heard the rabbit, the bicycle or both; or if the man was teasing me. The pipeline crew had just completed loading their equipment on some trailers in the state game lands parking lot when I passed through. I learned that they were from Perry County and traveled a lot working on the pipelines. As I left and walked on the roads toward Manada Gap, I still didn't know if I had heard the rabbit.

Just past Sleepy Hollow Road, Diane arrived with the second vehicle to take me back to the vehicle I had parked in Stony Valley. It was a great hike. I learned what "at your own risk" means and to carry a carabineer to suspend the backpack on cable bridges. I saw some fine views and talked with some nice people. I appreciated that Diane had come for me. We were going to dinner at Bob Evans on the way to get the other vehicle. What a nice ending for a great day!

So ended day six on the Horse-Shoe Trail.

Chapter
8

Night Walk on the
Horse-Shoe Trail.
(HST Map 9, March 20, 1999.)

Snow from the March 6, 1999 storm had receded from the ridges of the mountains on this section by Friday, March 19, 1999. The plan for Saturday was to stage one vehicle at Stony Creek Valley, hike from a drop off on PA Route 325 to the terminus of the Horse-Shoe Trail on the Appalachian trail, then to follow the HST to a suitable camp site and camp out. On the second day, the hike would be completed at the vehicle staged in Stony Creek Valley. The estimated distance was about 14 miles. Our son Michael and Ann, his wife, were hiking with me.

Parking the return vehicle in Stony Valley, at the same space along the narrow dirt road as used before for a departure point, I felt some pride that I had completed the hike south from here, across Second Mountain, during the last hike. A shiny new carabineer was clipped to the backpack, just in case it was needed to suspend the pack from a cable bridge, or whatever.

Diane and Tucker, our grandson, left us at the parking area adjacent the Appalachian Trail and Clark's Creek. The pile of mattresses and garbage was still there to welcome everyone using these areas. What a nice greeting!

Packing up, we waved our goodbyes and started the climb up Third Mountain to the Horse-Shoe Trail, about four miles distant. I encouraged Ann and Michael to take one of the pieces of limestone from a pile in the parking area to put in the mine drainage about half way to the HST. I took one also.

Changes in the landscape from two weeks ago were amazing. There was little snow left, except in areas shaded by rock formations or large boulders. The color in the hardwood trees had changed visibly and new growth on the leaf buds at the ends of the branches was noticeable. The air smelled of spring. Not the fragrant overwhelming aroma of millions of plants in full blossom, but the smell of subtle warmth and moisture from a fertile land. A faint yet powerful scent was in the air. A promise of the majesty and bounty of nature yet to come forth.

Reaching the site where the mine shaft penetrated the heart of the mountain, we placed our three limestone rocks in the acid drainage; a gesture more symbolic than functional.

Crossing the drainage field from the mine, I thought back to a time when I had splashed battery acid on a new pair of jeans at a service station where I worked after classes during high school. There was no obvious damage to the jeans at the time but after they were washed holes appeared where the acid had been splashed. Now I wondered if the strings which bound my boots together would rot and fall apart later if I got them wet? I tried to avoid getting my boots wet!

Reaching the intersection with the Horse-Shoe Trail was rewarding. I was relieved and grateful that there was no snow cover here, no winds, and that it was a pleasant day for a hike. I was also delighted for the company. After signing the trail register we started south and down the mountain, pausing for a happy photograph. (See Photograph 11) The trail descended over some rock formations on an old road, then went steeply down loose rock and soil to the valley between Third Mountain and Sharp Mountain. The area and views were fascinating and the descent was difficult, affirming the good choice I had made two weeks ago to turn back rather than to attempt this section alone, in heavy snow.

Approaching the bottom of the valley, it sounded like a train was coming toward us. The sound increased in volume as we descended. Gradually, I came to recognize that the sound was coming from below the ground, not from down the valley! The sound was not from a train, but possibly from water running below the surface of the boulder field below us. At the bottom of the valley the noise from below the ground was so loud that it was actually frightening.

Ruins of several stone structures were noted in this area. There is no indication of what these were. I would speculate they were abandoned due to the noise from below the ground which sounded like the entire valley should wash away at any moment!

Marking the ruins on the map, the words "Devil's Race Course" were noted. I wondered if the name had something to do with the noise from below the ground which sounded like a racing locomotive with a hundred freight cars in tow. Attributing the noise to ground water from snow melt rushing through the boulder field, I was never-the-less very pleased when we were moving up the far side of this valley away from the "Devil's Race Course" and Rattling Run. Hiking along Rattling Run Road, even uphill, is a nice walk. The trail is wide enough that we could all walk side by side and have a good conversation as we walked. There were no obstructions, and there was no doubt about where the trail was located.

Walking into the sunset, we looked for suitable areas to camp. There were many areas where excavations have been made in the top of the mountain and they all had standing water, with one exception. The exception was a nice grassy area which looked like an excellent camp site. We walked over to inspect this area and it had pipes coming from the ground. After some consideration, we speculated that the site was either an area where a fuel tank leaked and was being cleaned up, or that the pipes were mine vents. Since the trail was so nice we decided to continue forward, even though it was getting dark, and find another site where we could light the camp stoves without fear of being blown into orbit from ignition of an underground fuel source!

A large open field was just ahead. The trail markers indicated that the HST went into the field. A tractor road ran along the perimeter of the field. We could see no Horse-Shoe Trail markers beyond the one at the edge of the field. The trail was not very used in this area. We followed the tractor road around the circumference of the field to the access road on the opposite side of the clearing and found this to be the Horse-Shoe Trail.

The moon was out, it was a clear, quiet, night and the trail was good. "It's less than five miles to the vehicle and it's mostly downhill. What do you want to do? Ann?"

"Let's go for it."

"Michael?"

"I agree."

"It's unanimous," I announced. We continued along the access road and soon came to the radio and microwave towers at the apex of the valley between the tops of Second and Third Mountains. The view of lights illuminating the suburbs west of Harrisburg from the area near base of the eastern most tower was incredible. We stopped here for about twenty minutes and enjoyed this view of the lights from the darkness. We were aliens, examining a distant civilization. Photographs were attempted, but did not develop. There probably was not adequate exposure time with the camera available. Michael introduced me to "Power Bars"during our stop. Considerable grams of protein, carbohydrate, vitamins and minerals were in every bite. The taste was like that of cactus water: Great, if you are dying of dehydration.

Continuing west and descending on a good road, Michael and Ann were concerned with missing the turn back to the east. I shared with them my observation from the past week's hike that we would intersect the Buckeye Pipe Line clearing b where the trail turned and that it would be very obvious. They accepted this but still searched the trees for blazes, occasionally finding one, with their flashlights. I tried to avoid looking at the illuminated areas and losing my natural night vision, which takes more than 20 minutes to become functional after exposure to light.

The east turn of the trail was spotted with the flashlights. As the trail turned into the woods and narrowed, I used the flashlight also to avoid any obstacles as we wound our way down and onto the abandoned railroad bed and to the vehicle. The vehicle was a welcome site and we discussed stopping at a fast food facility on the way home for some real, and less concentrated, food.

After burgers, milk shakes and french fries, we came to the assistance of a gentleman who had stopped along Route 322 for gas and could not start the loaned car. The service station had closed and abandoned him. He was on a church related trip, traveling from Philadelphia to Erie. We had jumper cables and started his car for him with an admonition to not turn it off until he got where he was going.

Taking the cellular phone from the protective holder in the backpack, we called home. "Hi Honey, we're coming home." The signal probably was transmitted from the tower we had just sat under admiring night views of Harrisburg!

Walking at night is nice on well defined, clear trails. The views at night are different than during the day and from a different perspective. The smells and sounds are also different. The fact that there are not many areas visible from here where there are no artificial lights at night is obvious.

A flashlight is a good piece of equipment and a spare battery for long walks at night is useful but take a red lens to protect your night vision.

Photographs did not turn out at night with a disposable camera.

Power Bars are great to carry for protein and carbohydrates but do not come close to a fresh burger for taste.

The cellular phone was again very convenient, where it could be used, and we did a good deed for a stranger. It was an enjoyable conversation and a great hike!

So ended day seven and night one on the Horse-Shoe Trail.

Chapter 9

Rerouted!

(HST Map 9, March 25, 1999.)

Completion of Horse-Shoe Trail maps became milestones since each map represented 1/9 of the total trail. Completion of the three miles of Dauphin County remaining between the parking area off Furnace Road and East Appalachian Trail Road would complete HST maps 8 and 9.

Completion of these two maps was a double milestone and I set out on the late afternoon of Thursday March 25, 1999, to achieve this objective.

Parking at Furnace Road and Manada Creek, I leashed Diane's dog, Shelby, who we had adopted from the Humane Society, strapped on the light gear belt and followed the yellow blazes into the woods along Manada creek. The woods envelope the trail along this stream. The first tenth of a mile was very relaxing and refreshing. Coming to a bottom area, I was appalled at the ruts which had been cut into the trail by vehicles. The puddles of water and mud were more than boot top deep and the trail surface had been obliterated!

Carrying the dog around the mud, to avoid domestic stress, and following the blazes I progressed slowly north. Soon, the "old beeches and hemlocks" gave way to a mass of branches and lumbering debris. There were no more blazes to be found and no trail to follow in the tangled mass of branches and tree limbs.

With the map and compass, I plotted a course to the top of the next ridge, where the trail was supposed to follow the ridge for about a mile, thinking this would be easy to find. I struck out on a compass heading through the brush and branches, soon crossing Manada Bottom Road. It was very difficult to negotiate the tangled masses of branches, tree sections, and underbrush. Stopping frequently to guide Shelby's leash through obstructions, read the compass, look for the trail and, to carry her over especially difficult areas, I made very slow progress. It got dark as we crested the ridge and dogs started barking in the distance.

The flashlight was used to search for blazes, and the trail register which the trail guide indicated was at the top of the ridge. We, Shelby and I, were at the top of the ridge, and now on map 9, but where on the top of the ridge I could not tell. I found no blazes or register. "Shelby" didn't say whether she had detected them or not!

Children's voices could now be heard with the barking of dogs ahead. Locating the trail was not going well. Not wanting to cause a panic by walking out of the woods into someone's back yard at night, or anxiety for Diane, we returned to Manada Bottom Road by compass, using the flashlight because of the underbrush and branches, then called home and followed this road back to Furnace Road and the vehicle.

Confused, and wanting to see how badly I had been lost, I drove back to the intersection of the HST with Manada Bottom Road. The Horse Shoe was still there! I continued driving and went around to East Appalachian Trail road. Turning left from Route 443 toward the Fishing Creek Elementary School, I looked for blazes. The blazes which were right here at this intersection two weeks ago were gone! I stopped and examined the pole which I distinctly remembered because of the turn indicated there. The blazes had been covered with tar! Looking carefully at some of the other poles along the roads provided confirmation that the trail markings had been removed! Where had the trail gone? I understood my confusion. The trail had been removed in the two weeks since I had last been there! Driving home, surprised and somewhat bewildered, I wondered what had happened.

Another surprise waited at home, this one more pleasant. In the mailbox were back copies of the "BLAZE," the official publication of the Horse-Shoe Trail Club. The copies had been sent because I had so enjoyed the hikes close to home that we had joined the HST club as family members a week or so before.

Reading the "Blaze," I found that the HST would be relocated in the area I had just returned from, and showed the new route. The notice was several months old! What timing. What a relief!

"Shelby" and I had achieved the milestone of completing map 8 and we had an interesting walk. There was frustration because of the condition of the damaged trail, and my expectations. Rather than tall trees, we were challenged with obstructions. The walk was not a total failure and we were not lost in the woods. There was some good news.

Today I learned what happens when a trail is relocated. I also learned several important benefits of belonging to the trail club for the trail one is hiking. The information which is received is very valuable in keeping the trail guide up to date and knowing where to look for the trail if one is astray. The newsletter also provides the ability to contribute to the quality of the trail resource through participation in working hikes. In addition, social events and organized hikes are announced. Organized hikes reduce the cost of access and return, provide interesting company, and increase the safety of the hikes for everyone participating. Membership in the Horse-Shoe Trail Club was, and remains, a very good investment for us. If you are interested in hiking, consider membership and participation in a trail organization. If you pay attention to the sheer number of trail relocations, you will also get an understanding of the value of securing the property for a trail corridor. If you go out and walk or work on the trail, you will get an even greater appreciation for the cost of trail construction and disruption from trail relocations.

On April 5, 1999, Diane joined in inspecting this relocated section of the Horse-Shoe Trail described in the Blaze. We took a short walk from the intersection on Route 443 to the trail register so that I could officially sign in. We walked a mile or so on the new trail section and enjoyed this. We returned to the vehicle, never signing the register but enjoying the experience.

I returned with "Shelby" on April 7, 1999 and walked some of the relocated area north of the State Game Land parking area back to the east, but still did not find the trail register on this outing. (I did reach it eventually.)

The trail crews did a nice job of establishing the new corridor and it is much nicer than the initial experience in this area. Thank you for this.

So ended day eight, consisting of three evenings, on the Horse-Shoe Trail. Perhaps it was also a beginning, judging from Diane's smile in the relocated area.

Chapter 10

Humility!

(HST Map 6, April 3, 1999.)
(With Renee)

Renee, our daughter, is a pilot and was coming home for the weekend. "Bring a pack and we can take a hike while you are home,"I urged.

"Cool!" Was Renee's response.

Renee arrived at our home on Friday evening. We convinced Diane to drive us to our drop off point at PA Route 72 the next morning. We would park the return vehicle at the State Game Lands parking lot and then ride with Diane to the drop off point.

On Saturday we packed a lunch and departed as planned. It was a beautiful day with clear skies and temperatures in the mid 60's. At the drop off point, Renee and I dismounted, packed up and walked to and across route 72. Diane waved as she left to return home. The parking area near the gate at Route 72 was in use by eight vehicles. A busy day on the Horse-Shoe Trail I thought.

After a short distance, the HST turned into the forest on a nice path with a stone base and lots of oak leaves for cushion. This is a nice section of trail and we made good time ascending to the top of a gentle rise. The faint odor of skunk was in the air. We did not assume that the lingering odor was from a deer hunter or from a skunk's fatal encounter with a predator the evening before! We watched carefully for the source of this aroma as we negotiated our way between some fallen trees which had been cut for the trail to pass.

Happily, we did not encounter the skunk in person.

Descending from the top of the hill, erosion was obvious in the trail bed. Some of the stones which had been placed to direct water away from the trail had been removed and this contributed to the erosion. There were scrape marks on many of the stones in the trail and I wondered what was making them. Near the bottom of the hill I found a rectangular piece of plastic reflector about 3/8 inch wide by 4 inches long and pocketed it.

Climbing up the far side toward Governor Dick Park, there were several more of these reflective pieces, but about half way up the slope, a bicycle wheel reflector was found. I now understood that the other pieces of reflector must have broken from bicycle pedals as they struck the numerous stones along this stretch of trail.

Looking up at the sound of metallic scraping noises on rock above us, we saw two bicyclists approaching from above us on the trail. The front sprockets of their bicycles occasionally dragged on stones as they came down the many erosion dams in the trail. We waved and moved aside for the bicyclists to pass. They thanked us and rode past. I was amazed that the riders could negotiate this section of trail without dumping the bicycles. These riders did well and didn't appear to loose any mechanical parts as they passed. From the number of reflectors on the trail, other bike riders had not fared so well!

Near the top of this ascent a unique rock formation was visible to the right. We looked at it then continued on to the observation tower at Governor Dick Park.

Governor Dick, according to the Horse-Shoe Trail Guide, memorializes a slave who operated a charcoal burner in the area. He is said to have run away from his owner in 1796. The reward for his return was $20. I wondered what had happened to him.

Observing the view from the tower is worth the climb but no rapelling, the sign on the side of the tower reads.

Our son and his classmates were probably here!

Metal gridwork which now encloses the top of the tower makes rapelling very difficult from within the tower, even if one were so inclined. The ladders inside the tower are not as much fun to descend but much safer, since the fall is only six feet or so at each landing compared to the forty or fifty foot drop from the top of the tower. The view from this tower is worth the time and effort and changes with each season. The attractiveness of the view was obvious from the crowd of people in the area.

After crosing the paved road, I was surprised to see that almost every tree had been splattered with a circular yellow spot of paint about the same height as the blazes we were following. It looked like the entire forest was infected with yellow chicken pox! There was no easy way to identify the trail blazes from the yellow splatters of paint. We followed the road, which was wide enough to walk side by side and clearly visible. I wondered if the persons who marked the trees had ever heard of a contrast color? It would have been nice if the paint colors were something different than the yellow of the Horse-Shoe Trail blazes.

Exceptions were trees which had nesting cavities in them. There were no paint spots on them. I assumed this was to protect the habitat these cavities provided.

"Do you remember walking the AT where you put one foot down in North Carolina and the other foot down in Tennessee when you were very young?" I asked Renee as we hiked along at a very respectable pace.

"I wasn't there, was I?"

"That's my recollection," I responded, making a mental note to look for the photographs of the last time we took a hike together as a family when we returned home. Actually, I remembered that she put both of her tiny hands in my right hand and I hoisted her to my shoulders when she became tired, without really noticing the difference in weight of my day pack, during that series of hikes on the AT.

"I remember the water slides, and the cavern we were in when all of the lights went out! Was that the same trip?"

"Yes. Do you remember fishing with me in the Smoky Mountains after the storm that flooded the camp?"

"No, but I remember us all sleeping in the van in the storm. There was a padded board that you put between the front bucket seats for me to sleep on, Michael slept on the back seat, and you and Mom were in the back."

We had a great conversation as we hiked along. Our daughter, who I remember growing up from a small and fragile child through college and beyond, has matured. She remains kind and generous as ever and for this I am grateful.

We continued at a good pace and passed several more bicyclists, on the more level trail, going in the opposite direction. We also saw a woman riding a horse, crossing the field in front of us. There were several horse trailers in the parking lot for the State Game Lands near the road which led to Colebrook. We crossed the paved road and continued on a good, well marked, trail and through pleasant scenery. (Photograph 16)

Crossing the railroad grade and descending, we came to Conewago Creek. The swamp to the right was an urban sprawl area for ducks. There were nesting boxes every several yards across this swamp, or lake, and it was a very strange sight. It reminded me of a ten inch diameter birthday cake I once saw for a person celebrating their eighty something birthday. There were candles protruding in all directions and the candles were placed so close together that the cake resembled a heavy duty round scrub brush with large white flaming bristles; but no handle.

This swamp had so many bird boxes and poles protruding so close together, and in so many different directions, that it resembled the top of this cake; magnified about a thousand times!

The HST follows a nice path across the bottom lands and upward to the parking area. Reaching the parking lot I was winded. We had traveled the eight miles in about two and one half hours. As we placed our gear in the vehicle I was patting myself of the back for the great pace we had maintained when Renee announced: "We went four miles in two hours of hiking time, that's pretty slow."

I looked at the map again. Eight miles were clearly indicated.

"It looks more like eight miles according to the map," I observed.

"No, Dad, we only went four miles. See, my pedometer shows how far we walked. That's only two miles per hour. We went really slow."

I checked the map again, saw eight miles, and didn't argue. Having our youngest child walk my legs off and announce that we went really slow, as I was congratulating myself on the excellent pace, gave me a new perspective. It's called humility!

Perhaps the map is correct? Even so, I had learned that our daughter could hold her own pace, even with the pack, and was pleased with this knowledge. I wondered if her time at higher elevations when she is flying airplanes gave her a conditioning advantage in addition to her youth. "Let's go home and see if we can find those pictures," I suggested.

"Cool." Was Renee's response.

Today I learned humility, again. I observed the value of contrast colors demonstrated very clearly, saw some really great views, took some nice photographs, learned what caused scrape marks on some of the rocks and downed trees on the HST, and enjoyed the company of our daughter. It was a great hike.

So ended day 9 on the HST.

1. Swatara Creek

2. Sand Beach Road, Hershey, PA

3. View to North, Horse-Shoe Trail
S outh of Swatara Creek

4. View to Northeast, Horse-Shoe Trail
South of Swatara Creek

5. "Community Spirit"
Horse-Shoe Trail
passes between
Home and Shed

6. "White Out" In sheltered area.

7. "Use at your own risk!"
Cable Bridge at Stony Creek

8. Stony Valley and Stony Creek

9. Third Mountain from Buckeye
Pipeline, looking north.

10. Author at Second Mountain,
view to south.

11. "Happy Hikers, Ann & Michael,"
on the Horse-Shoe Trail

12. "Rerouted"

13. Newly constructed trail.

14. Diane and "Shelby"

15. Observation Tower at Governor Dick/Author

16. "Renee, Waiting for Dad"

17. Valley Forge

18. "Mile 0.0"

19. Trail Marker - 133 Miles to Home

20. Ann at abandoned bottling plant.

21. Corridor through industrial area.

22. Development and Relocation

23. HST beside, but not on, the road.

24. HST safely on the PA Turnpike Corridor

25. Sunset at Mile 11.8, Michael and Ann

26. Sunset at Mile 11.8 Michael and Dad

27. Trees against the sky.

28. Mile 11.8, Just about dark.

29. Nice Developments

30. Stone arch in field.

31. "Stone Ranch"

32. "Gravel Road"

33. "Dense Woods"

34. "Step Stones"

35. Blacked out blaze on bridge.

36. "The Drive Home," PA 322 and 72

37. "Cable Crossings" Ann, Michael, Author

38. "HST's Bridge to the 21st Century"

39. Horses at Warwick Park

40. "Primitive Methods of Working Stone"

41. "Old Stone House"

42. Lake with feeding fish.

43. French Creek Stone Dam

44. "Turtle"

45. Saint Paul's Church

46. "Mountain Laurel"

47. "Wheat Field"

48. "Iron Bridge over Railroad"

49. "Erosion"

50. Police helping runners, PA Route 10.

51. "Evergreen Plantation"

52. "Young Corn Field"

53. "Farm Pond"

54. "Halfway"

55. "Substation"

56. "Honeysuckle"

57. "Clear Cut"

58. "Ornamental Plants"

59. Muddy Middle Creek

60. "Mushroom Rock"

Chapter 11

Mile 0.0

(HST Map 1, May 19, 1999.)

The original plan for this day was to be on day four of six days on the Susquehannock Trail System (STS), about 250 miles to the northwest, but this was not to be. Using the Horse-Shoe Trail, mostly on weekends, as conditioning and shakedown hikes for myself and the equipment for six days of wilderness hiking resulted in completion of the western third of the Horse-Shoe Trail (HST) before the attempt on the STS, which had been aborted. That is another story.

At this point I wanted to complete something. I had thoroughly enjoyed most of the hiking on the Horse-Shoe Trail, with the exception of the ten miles of road in Dauphin County. Our son, Michael, and daughter-in-law, Ann, had hiked the Stony Valley, Second Mountain, and Third Mountain parts of the HST with me and were convinced to join me in driving to the origin of the HST and walking back toward home. Taking two vehicles and staging one at an end point and the other at the start point, we would leap frog the vehicles at comfortable intervals, travel light, and see how much of the HST we could take in at a leisurely pace during our remaining vacation.

On May 19, 1999, we were going to start from Valley Forge National Park (Photograph 17), the origin of the Horse-Shoe Trail, also referred to as "Mile 0.0" (Photograph 18). The day was cloudy and threatened rain. We left one vehicle at Route 113, the end of HST map 1, about 13 miles from Valley Forge National Park. Driving to the park was a typical urban rush hour scene with all lanes bumper to bumper. Road signs must have been removed because there was no indication of where to leave Route 202 to get onto Route 422. We toured several local neighborhoods attempting to reach Route 422 and Valley Forge. It would have been better to use the turnpike than to use the local roads!

Reaching Valley Forge, things were better. The rangers were very considerate and supportive of our plan to park one vehicle there, then to return for it after the parking lot had closed. They gave us permission to park in an area where the vehicle would be accessible when we returned, assuming we made it back! The rangers also provided a map of the park showing the origin of the Horse-Shoe Trail, and directed us to the locaton where we should park to reach the trail.

Valley Forge National Park is a treasure. The grounds are well kept, the facilities are accessible, modern, and well staffed and the restorations are very well done for the purpose they serve. Take an extra day and visit here. It is a very interesting historical site that is a pleasure to tour.

We toured Valley Forge National Park, on the loop road, by vehicle, and decided to return the next morning for photographs of the various sites since in was very overcast. This is a most thought provoking area. Looking at the primitive shelters here one can imagine the hardships previous generations went through during the Revolutionary War. One observation was just how much effort and human sacrifice went into gaining independence from a government that previous generations didn't like. I wondered whether their actions and sacrifices would ever be necessary again. This led to the realization that only the firearms available to the Colonists made the success of the Revolution possible. Following this awareness was the question of whether an event such as the Revolutionry War would ever be possible again, if conditions became so oppressive, in view of the current climate of weapons control. The tour of Valley Forge National Park was worth the journey.

Things were definitely looking up as we debated rain gear, left the vehicle, walked to the marker for mile 0.0 and posed for photographs. The monument reads:

"START OF THE HORSE-SHOE TRAIL IN PENNA
VALLEY FORGE TO APPALACHIAN TRAIL ON STONY MT.
121 MILES - THROUGH CHESTER BERKS LANCASTER
LEBANON and DAUPHIN COUNTIES
THIS MARKER ERECTED 1972
BY THE HORSE-SHOE TRAIL CLUB, INC 1935
IN MEMORY OF HENRY N. WOOLMAN, FOUNDER"

We carried water, snacks in our pockets, map, compass, two cameras, flashlights, and a trail guide. No packs! I was so exuberant to be without the heavy pack of the past three days that I exclaimed: "Tie my feet down, someone, or I'm going to float away!" (I was also 15 pounds lighter in body weight.)

A feeling of continuity was experienced at being here. I photographed the HST marker, which is quite nice. It was good to be here with some of my family. I had a sense of accomplishment. It was almost like completing the borders of a thousand piece jig saw puzzle. All the boundaries were now defined and we were working on the middle. It wasn't completed, but we had now seen both ends and where the pieces fit. I thought also, that I probably felt like someone who makes a pilgrimage; after all the travel it is nice to see the object which symbolizes the effort, even an object as physically small as Plymouth Rock, which was a serious disappointment!

Leaving from Valley Forge about 5 PM, rain started to fall intermittently. Accepting that we would be wet, we set out following the yellow blazes and were soon surprised at what a lovely trail has been preserved in this area and the nice environment and views available just a mile or so from the expressway. The trail was so well located and marked that it was actually easier to walk from Valley Forge than it had been to drive to it. I also believe it was quicker! Although we did not record the driving and walking times to state this as a fact, all of us had this perception.

"Horse-Shoe Trail, Hershey 133 miles," the trail marker read as we hiked along Valley Creek Trail on a wide gravel path. (Photograph 19) The houses in the area were very old and well preserved. It is an easy hike and an interesting area.

Soon we came to some ruins with a concrete cave opening into the hillside which had a culvert transporting water to the opening. We explored this and read in the trail guide that it was an old bottling plant. Very interesting. I wondered what was bottled here. The stone construction was fascinating and well preserved. We spent some time exploring this site. (Photograph 20)

Continuing through a wooded area, we passed houses on both sides of the trail with very nice landscaping and numerous flowers and plants in full bloom. The sights and scents of the numerous flowers and blossoms were a special treat.

Winding between industrial sites, public facilities, private homes and several roads, the Horse-Shoe Trail in this area is an example of what good planning and cooperation between citizens, industry and local government can accomplish. In this area the beauty of wilderness, nature, landscaping, and architecture demonstrated the cooperation of citizens of the community. The essence of this community is manifest in the path which follows the center of the Horse-Shoe Trail corridor, not more than ten feet wide, through the heart of this community. (Photograph 21) This accomplishment is inspiring and provides a very favorable impression of the local community, their planners, and their builders.

Continuing on, we came to more developing areas. Some had the trail running parallel to, but not on, the paved roads. This was considerate and enjoyable. At mile 4 there was one stretch of road where the trail was actually on the pavement. This is near a development across from and west of Chautanqua Trail (an access road.) "Spec Homes from the low 700's, only one left'" the sign read. (Photograph 22)

Hopefully there will be a corridor for the trail here when the development is completed. The homes are nice and it is a pleasant area.

Agriculture was observed. After passing from the highly populated areas through some very old wooded areas, we gradually encountered farms, open fields and meadows. The trail runs along the roads in many places here, but there is room to travel off the paved road. (Photograph 23) The animals came over to visit as we passed, enjoying the views of the well maintained farms and buildings.

I remembered a course in "Economic Geography." The author must have walked this part of the Horse-Shoe Trail! The theories espoused in the text were being demonstrated here.

Just beyond Phoenixville Road was a storm water trench about ten feet deep with relatively steep sides and too wide to leap across, even without the pack. Climbing carefully down the side I noted, with gratitude, that someone had placed a 4"x4" board across the bottom of the trench. This bridge was just above the water and securely anchored on each end. We crossed this narrow bridge without soaking our feet with appreciation for the bridge builder.

Crossing a stream on step stones then walking through some woods, we came into an open field with an old, unpruned and disfigured apple tree standing alone in some high weeds. It was getting dark and the tree looked lonely and abandoned. This was a good setting for a ghost story!

Moving through the field of hay, on a farm lane, we soaked our feet. The water from the hay, overhanging the road, ran into the tops of the boots as we walked through. It had not rained much where we had hiked until now, but obviously it had rained more significantly here. The smell of the humidity and the promise of mist or fog to come was in the air and lightning bugs began to illuminate the wood line at the edge of the field.

Traveling along the Pennsylvania Turnpike Corridor was a unique experience. (Photograph 24) The Horse-Shoe Trail runs on the hillside above the turnpike through a tunnel formed by tall trees and relatively dense underbrush. This experience was like walking through one of the turnpike tunnels. There was one real difference: Here, if you wanted to, you could turn and walk out through the walls! Not so in the turnpike tunnels. From this area turnpike can be heard, but not seen when the leaves are on the trees.

Further along, at the point where the HST turns south, there is a view of the turnpike travel lanes in both directions. The sights, sounds, and smells of the turnpike are experienced here, but from a remote perspective. It is sort of like watching a professional baseball game from a tall building outside the stadium. You have permission to be here, you are experiencing the game, but you aren't participating in the action! This is very different. We stopped and took in this experience for a few moments.

Darkness was upon us at the vista at mile 11.8! The sky was streaked with various colored cloud formations, back lighted by the setting sun. At the edge the large field a nice silhouette of the ridges in the background was visible. We stopped and took photographs. They are one of a kind - they actually developed.

As darkness more thoroughly enveloped the world and the sky turned dark, lightning bugs put on a dazzling display across the field. The smell of the wet hay field, of various plants in blossom, and the mist now rising in the field became more distinct and pleasant. Insects began a chorus of sound which varied in volume, frequency, tone and distance. I looked up and saw one or two stars and, perhaps, the space station Mir reflecting sunlight. I wondered if the astronauts missed the sounds and smells of earth or the views of little things, such as lightning bugs. The computer enhancement equipment on board most observing satellites would probably show the illuminated area from below the lightning bugs in sharp detail, but the bug's shell would block the clear view of the light emitting phosphor which was so dazzling in front of us this evening, even without enhancement technology. What an amazing, wonderful, fragrant and beautiful world!

With our feet soaked, from walking through the tall hay which overhangs the trail, flashlights were used to negotiate our way through the woods and to Horse-Shoe Trail Road. At the waterfall, beside the road, the Horse-Shoe Trail's yellow arrowhead was on a tree behind the water. It was in the mist and illuminated by crossing flashlight beams piercing the darkness. I photographed the arrowhead to preserve this memorable sight. It didn't expose properly on the film, but the image is still in my memory.

The return vehicle was waiting at Route 113. We put on dry shoes, returned to the first vehicle, then stopped to tell the Park Rangers we were back. That night we camped at the McIntosh Inn.

Today I learned that the Horse-Shoe Trail corridor, near Valley Forge, is a truly remarkable accomplishment. I enjoyed the company of our son and daughter-in-law and am pleased that they do so well together. I experienced invigorating sights, smells, sounds and thoughts. I truly enjoyed Valley Forge National Park and the courtesy of the Park Rangers. I appreciated the sacrifice and hardship which others endured to bring us the freedom we enjoy in our nation today. With every mile I hiked, more appreciation for those responsible for hosting, establishing and maintaining the Horse-Shoe Trail developed. This trail is a major achievement.

We had completed an entire map, 13 miles, of the Horse-Shoe Trail in about five hours, some in the dark.

I learned today that one night in a motel is about the same price as a pretty good tent, although the motel remains the more comfortable choice.

So ended day 10 and night 2 on the Horse-Shoe Trail.

Chapter 12

Convenience, Developments, Woods, Fields and Fun.

(HST Map 2, May 20, 1999.)

(PA Route 113 to Coventryville Road, with Michael and Ann.)

The plan for Thursday, May 20, 1999, was to park one vehicle at Coventryville Road, drive back to Route 113, then to hike the area between. Again, we would be traveling light, with the exception of the water remaining in our boots from walking through the wet hay fields the evening before.

Departing the MacIntosh Inn, we stopped at uncle Bob's; "Bob Evans" restaurant that is, for breakfast before our hike. One of the things I had missed most during the three days just spent in more remote areas, where we had backpacked, was coffee in the morning. Because of the weight of the equipment to prepare real coffee, and not caring for instant coffee, I had forsaken the daily consumption of coffee. I missed coffee and mentioned this on my second or third morning of abstinence. Since we had left from home yesterday, I had brewed a fresh pot of coffee and had some with breakfast the day before. Joining Ann and Michael at the Bob Evans restaurant I noted, with pleasure and appreciation, that Ann and Michael had already ordered coffee for me and it was steaming in the cup, just poured, as I sat down.

Convenience is a hallmark of the trail in this area. There are hotels, motels, restaurants, department stores, libraries, sporting goods stores, grocery stores - any kind of store you need is in the Valley Forge area. We were as much tourists as visitors from New England or other countries. My cost for the hotel room, breakfast, telephone and a disposable camera was about $110.00. Three entire days in more remote areas cost $26.00. This included $14.00 for a camp site when we stayed at the Lyman Run State Park and $12.00 for insect repellent at the only park side convenience store within 35 miles. Convenience has a price; but it is nice. The coffee and breakfast were great!

Returning to Valley Forge National Park, we took photographs, then departed for our hike. It was sunny with a gentle breeze as we parked the return vehicle at a parking area where Coventryville Road crosses French Creek. Fish were visible in the water below the bridge as we changed vehicles and drove to PA Route 113, north of Opperman's Corner.

Sluggish from the heavy breakfast, we started hiking on a paved road. For a short distance in this area there was little room on the shoulder of the road to dodge oncoming vehicles. Fortunately for us, most of the drivers were very courteous and attempted to make room for us to continue safely without diving over the fences along the road.

Rounding a turn in the road we saw two men installing turf on a newly developed lawn. It was amazing how the bare soil turned into a beautiful lawn after unrolling the turf from a truck and spraying it with water. Magic! We talked with one of the men while the other moved the truck, then continued up a rise and into a developed area with very nice homes and acres of blooming flowers, shrubs, and trees. The homes in each development were of different ages and styles, but all were well kept and it was very pleasant walking through the developments. (Photograph 29)

A stone arch was in a field to the right of the trail, perhaps covering a spring? Perhaps the arch was a former bridge which had once supported the road over the small creek we were now crossing on the new road? (Photograph 30)

Stone structures prevailed in this area. A stone barn, stone house, stone landscaping walls and stone terraces were observed on the left side of the trail. What a unique architectural achievement this was. For me, this was one of the most striking views on the entire trail. Using all native stone, except for the roofing, the entire construction flowed gracefully drawing my eyes from one end of the property to the house at the apex of the constructed area. I enjoyed the view of this property and appreciated the designer and workers who had created this marvelous effect. My limited camera equipment did not do justice to the view. (Photograph 31)

Stopping at the end of a development, we removed our boots and let our feet dry for a few moments while we had lunch and enjoyed the view from the curb. We changed our socks which had become wet from our still soaked boots, then hung the wet socks on our gear to dry as we walked. I was pleased that I had not developed blisters from the wet socks. The investment in wool blend hiking socks was worth the time, effort and expense.

Deep woods greeted us with cool shade which was a relief from the heat of the paved development roads. Leaving the woods, we came onto a gravel lane which we followed along a field. Fields and farms were more frequent now as we continued our hike, stopping from time to time to take photographs of the landscape. (Photograph 32)

Numerous vistas were on this entire section of the trail. While not a "Vista" that warrants a special notation in the trail guide, there were numerous places where the views across a field, from a ridge, or from a road crossing, provided a very nice view in one direction or another. This kept the walk interesting.

Passing through dense woods (Photograph 33) we could hear the sounds of traffic. Route 100 was just ahead. Crossing between traffic, we continued up a driveway, then through woods and fields, pausing frequently to admire the numerous views before us and to catch our breath, mostly mine, in this area.

Crossing numerous small creeks on step stones (Photograph 34) was a fun experience as was enjoying the views, architecture, farms, woods, developments and landscaping so diverse in this section of the HST.

We came to the "Magnificent View," aptly described in the trail guide. We took several photographs in this area and agreed with the impression expressed by the author of the trail guide.

At a small swamp the trail was badly torn up by horses. The trail base constrction would not support their weight and the horses had sunk a foot or so into the soft trail resulting in deep mud and difficult walking. Once we moved uphill a few yards, the horse tracks were no longer noticeable and we followed the trail along the ridge line and through the woods, coming out at French Creek Elementary School. The resemblance of the French Creek Elementary School to the Fishing Creek Elementary School, just off Route 443 in Dauphin County, and also on the Horse-Shoe Trail, was striking. They may have been built to the same plan and used the same materials. From the road in front of the school, we could see our return vehicle at the base of the hill and we started in that direction.

A farmer was cultivating a field to the east side of Coventryville Road. We watched as the spring loaded equipment bounced over several rocks, then reset. I was very impressed with this. The tractor was pulling three sets of cultivators and never needed to slow down to prevent equipment damage. The equipment was designed for this type of field and worked much better than what I had watched struggle to get through the fields in my younger years. Technology in action.

At the vehicle, we noticed that a yellow blaze on the south end of the bridge had been painted over with tar. (Photograph 35)

Checking the trail guide we noted that the Horse-Shoe Trail did not cross this bridge any longer. We also noted that there was another cable bridge about four tenths of a mile ahead. (Note: Since hiking this section of trail, I was heart broken to learn that the cable bridge has been removed during September or October, 1999, and the Horse-Shoe Trail now is routed on the road again, unless you don't mind wading through knee to hip deep water to cross here.)

Deciding to forego the convenience of the hotel, we chose to drive home, visit with the rest of our family, and attempt to complete map 2 of the HST the following day.

Passing Route 100, the route to the PA turnpike, we realized that tomorrow we would be one turnpike exit closer to completing our journey to Hershey. This simple fact pleased us. We had walked twenty two miles or so in two days just hiking along and enjoying the diverse and attractive scenery. In the two days we had not seen another hiker on the trail, although the trail was certainly well used and many pleasant neighbors and landowners greeted us as we passed.

Driving home from PA turnpike exit 20, to the west, I saw one of the nicest views to date: The vista at the intersection of PA Routes 72 and 322. I made a note to return very early some morning to take photographs of this area, and did. (Photograph 36)

Today I learned that one remembers the sequence and scenery on the trail better when you are the lead hiker, and enjoyed the family presence, diverse scenery, smells, and progress.

So ended day 11 on the Horse-Shoe Trail. It was a great hike!

Chapter
13

Warwick Park!
(HST Map 2, May 21, 1999.)
Coventryville Road to Pa Route 345

The plan for today was for Michael, Ann and I to start from home, travel to French Creek State Park with two vehicles, leave the recovery vehicle along PA Route 345, then return to the parking area at the crossing of French Creek by Coventryville Road, to depart from there.

At French Creek the fish were again visible in the water below the bridge and we watched them for a few moments.

Facing into the current, the fish appeared to be watching for food. I had once read in an outdoor magazine that fish flee from the shadow of fishermen. Since the sun was east of the bridge, it was decided to test the validity of information in that article. Standing on the western side of the bridge, I extended my arm to point the shadow of my hand at several different fish. The fish, without exception, fled before the shadow of my pointing finger even came close to them! I was surprised that they detected the shadow behind them and moved so quickly. Based on this very limited observation, it was noted that the information in the article may have been correct.

We traveled light, taking a sandwich, some snacks, water, compass, maps, spare socks, cameras and the trail guide. I remembered to take the carabineer to secure my equipment belt to the cable bridge, if needed, and we followed the tarred out blazes from the bridge back to the yellow blazes of the Horse-Shoe Trail just below French Creek Elementary School and turned west into the fields and woods.

The view along the past day's hike, and this section of trail, reminded me of walking along Skyline Drive in northern Virginia but on a somewhat smaller scale - the ridges and valleys here are not of the same magnitude. To the north, a ridge of hills dominated the skyline in the distance. In the valley, the fields, the farms and landscaping around the houses were colored with the full assortment of spring blossoms. The views and fragrances were very distracting to walking. I could stand here for hours and enjoy the scenery.

Listening to Michael and Ann discuss which areas would be the best location for a home along the trail, I gained an understanding of why there is development pressure along the corridor. I shared their enthusiasm for wanting to have a home with this view and environment, but understand that the view and environment change when each additional home is constructed. Remembering the magnificent architecture of the stone structures observed the day before, and how the trail was attractively routed between various developments in the Valley Forge area, I realized that the construction of homes does not have to destroy an environment, although it will certainly alter it. Design of developments, industrial complexes and individual homes can result in a beautiful community with a friendly and enjoyable environment, provided some plans are made and followed before building.

At the end of the row of pine trees along the field, we came to a woods with large trees, cool shadows and bright areas of sunlight illuminating the stream bank and a cable bridge! There were only two cable bridges on the entire Horse-Shoe Trail and these were a mini-adventure in and of themselves. I was delighted that I wasn't wearing a forty or fifty pound backpack for this one! A short briefing was given Michael and Ann on crossing the cables. Their exuberance demonstrated that they were as excited about this crossing as I was, and both posed for photographs of their crossings. I also posed. (Photograph 37, a,b,c. "Cable Crossings")

Putting my recyclable (versus disposable) camera in a plastic bag, I threw it across the creek to Michael. The camera hit the bank above him and rolled down. It was so light that the impact was negligible and the camera worked fine even after hitting the dirt. This was evidenced by my picture on the cable bridge.

Crossing this cable bridge was much more pleasant for me than crossing the one in Stony Valley with the heavy backpack. I changed technique, placing one hand on each of the upper cables and walking on the lowest one, facing straight ahead. Rather than crossing sideways and using two hands on one cable, I slid my hands along the two cables as I crossed, tightening my grip when I moved my feet, and stopping briefly when there was excessive movement in the cables. There were no major rocking motions, no strain on my arms, or twisting of the cables. Did these cables have more tension? Was the load better centered above the cable? I concluded that the fact that the load was better centered above the bottom cable was a factor in a better crossing.

We followed the blazes between the trunks of large trees along a pleasant section of trail on the banks of the south branch of French Creek. I stopped to examine the design and construction of the bridge which carries Mt. Pleasant Road over the creek. The span was about eighty feet long and features a graceful arch to distribute the load to concrete abutments at each end. The bridge is positioned above the surrounding land, providing some protection from flood damage by providing for flood waters to flow around the bridge rather than covering it and subjecting the sides of the span to the extreme pressures which can build up when debris backs water up on one side of a bridge. Interesting concepts and construction were observed here.

During Hurricane Agnes, in 1972, this and hundreds of other small rural bridges were washed out in Pennsylvania. The new design has incorporated most of the lessons learned and the new structure is definitely a bridge which should last into the new millennium. "The bridge to the 21st century is on the Horse-Shoe Trail!" (Photograph 38)

Entering Warwick Park, we hiked through woods on a nice dirt road. The road neared a clearing and from just inside the wood line we observed Eastern Blue Birds which were apparently nesting in the boxes placed along the clearing, near some picnic areas. I attempted to get a close up photograph of one of these brilliant blue backed and yellow bellied birds. I reached a distance within about 25 feet from the box before the bird flew away. The picture is there, but does not do justice to the brilliant colors of this bird.

The trail next led us to a platform with stairs on either end. This platform made a great observation deck. We enjoyed the view of the park and the ridges visible to the north from this structure. Reading the trail guide, we found that this platform was a historic bridge which had been relocated.

The blazes marking the HST disappeared at the edge of the mowed area of the park lawn. We saw posts, which apparently marked the park boundary, but no more blazes. Following the park boundary, we looked at each tree for a yellow blaze without success. Coming to a road, we followed this north, hoping to find the trail where it left the park. It was close to noon and some park workers were coming up the road on a maintenance vehicle. They waved at us and we waved back. We photographed some horses which were in a pasture along the west side of the road. (Photograph 39) About one quarter mile further down the road, we found a yellow blaze on the end of a stone bridge which had been tarred over. This was somewhat frustrating.

Turning back, we returned up the hill continuing to search for the yellow blazes, which mark the trail, without success. The park office was to the west. We decided to stop at the park office and ask for directions.

Park staff were in the process of having lunch when we entered the office lunch room and asked for direction. "Can you help us find the Horse-Shoe Trail?" I asked.

"Did you the white posts with the yellow tops?"

"Yeah?" I answered as a question.

"Those are the trail markers."

"Oh. I didn't realize that. We were looking for blazes."

"The trail comes back up just behind the office at the end of the driveway. Here, I'll show you," one of the men offered, leaving his lunch.

"That's alright," I protested. "Please finish your lunch, we can find it."

"No bother at all" the man persisted, turning around. The name on his name tag was the same as the last name of the Chemistry teacher who taught Diane and I in high school. I had to ask. "Do you know Weinels from Weinel's Crossroad, Pennsylvania?" I asked.

"I 'm from Weinel's Crossroad."

"Do you know Charlie?"

"Yes, that's my father! Where do you know him from?"

"Well, in 1964, your father was a chemistry teacher at Kiski Area Senior High School. My wife and I were both in his class."

"No way!" He exclaimed.

I described his father, the distinctive ties he wore, where he taught, and other details of our relationship as teacher and student. I showed him the scar on my hand where a chemistry experiment to generate hydrogen gas from acid and marble chips had turned into a fiasco when one of my classmates had struck a match to light a cigarette while his father was out of the room, detonating the hydrogen gas. The resulting explosion burst the hydrogen generator bottle and blew the thistle tube and rubber stopper into the ceiling. Fragments of the tube had cut my hand, which I had brought up instinctively to cover my face, coming down from the ceiling.

"I remember my father talking about that. He was really upset that happened!"

"Well, I was upset too, but not at your dad. I was upset with the one who struck the match. I also appreciated that we all had wrapped the bottles in a fabric to protect against bursting the generators and were using bottles with rubber stoppers rather than with screw on lids."

We talked for several minutes and I wrote down current information on his father, gave him a business card and asked him to tell his father that I said hello. I couldn't wait to tell Diane who I had met on our hike! We signed into the trail log at the end of the park office driveway and continued on our way. I made a note to myself to attempt to secure some of the yellow directional arrows that I saw on the trail, or some yellow horse shoes, to provide to Warwick Park to attach to the posts, so that later hikers would not have the same confusion and frustration with the different markers that we encountered. The loss of direction had a bright side!

We went through more nice woods, crossed a small creek, and climbed up to Hill Road which we followed to Route 23.

Entering the woods at the State Game Lands 43 on a nice trail, I took notice of numerous, evenly spaced, markings on the granite rock formations in the area. There were holes about 3/4 of an inch in diameter in neat rows along the edges of many of the larger stone slabs. There was a definite pattern here!

Were these marks where the stone slabs had been sectioned with wooden plugs? This was something I had read about in a history book - "Primitive Methods of Working Stone," or something to that effect - but had never observed in use. To quarry granite or slate, workers would reportedly drill a row of narrow holes into the edge of a slab to a uniform depth. The holes would be cleaned and dry hardwood plugs would be driven into the holes with a wooden mallet until the plug bottomed out. Once all of the plugs had been inserted, they were soaked with water several times per day, and kept covered with a wet cloth to keep them wet. Swelling of the wooden plugs created pressure from water being absorbed into the pores of the wood. The pressure of the swelling wood, I believe the process which generates this pressure was called "turgor," then splits the rock. If done properly, the rock breaks cleanly along the line of the wooden plugs in several days. Was this what created the markings we were observing? I thought this to be the case and was amazed that there was evidence that the information I had read in some obscure book was probably close to being accurate, again. (Photograph 40)

Surprise! Two hikers were approaching us from the west. These were the first people we had seen actually hiking on the trail since we had left Valley Forge. "Hi there! How are you doing?"

"OK." They weren't carrying any gear.

"Are you going far?"

"No, just back to St. Pete's."

"You are the only two people we have seen actually walking this trail and we are in our third day from Valley Forge. Do you mind if we take your picture?"

"Sure." They both smiled, and sort of shrugged, while I took their picture. We chatted for a few minutes and departed in opposite directions.

A "River of Rocks," per the trail guide, winds through this area. The rocks were very fascinating and the trail was good in this area. There were no low spots at all!

Following the abandoned corridor of the Reading Railroad, we examined how the drainage was accomplished for the rail bed. There was no erosion or settling where the drainage system was open and functional. Where the drains, which passed under the railroad bed, were obstructed, water had run over the top of the low area of the railroad bed and erosion resulted. The erosion damage was in relation to the degree of obstruction in the drainage system. More blockage resulted in greater erosion damage on the trail surface. In addition, the sides of the railroad bed were showing evidence of collapse where the water had backed up and softened the base material. This reminded me of the erosion on the section of the Appalachian Trail from PA Route 325 to the wounded mountain, before the junction of the Horse-Shoe Trail. Drainage and base material appear to be critical factors in both railroad and hiking trail construction, based on my observations of these areas.

Further along the railroad bed, we saw a modern quarry operation on the left side. I don't think they use wooden pegs to cut the stone any longer based on the hum of machinery coming from the building and the smooth granite slabs on pallets beside the building.

Leaving the railroad bed after a mile or more, we came to a crystal clear, cool and pretty creek. The banks of this creek were torn up from the horses where the soil was soft. The smell of the water was nice and I paused to drink some of the water from my canteen. It was tempting to drink directly from this creek but I no longer feel safe doing this. Regardless of how refreshing the water appears and smells, and how remote the area, there is a real risk of problems from this action. I remember when the quality of the water was generally safe and it was acceptable to drink from sources such as springs and creeks, like this one, and I mourn the increasing loss of these refreshing and sustaining sources of water to parasites and contamination.

Several nice views entertained us as we went along fields, through woods and across Pine Creek. After turning south on Harmonyville Road, a very old, weathered, but well preserved stone house was to the west; sheltered in the valley. This was an interesting house and I speculated on the history it had seen. There was a lot of character showing on this house and the yard. I used my last exposure on the recyclable camera to photograph it. (Photograph 41)

Checking the trail log, I noted that the cable bridge over Pine Creek was no longer used. I regretted this, for I thoroughly relished the cable bridges. If you are interested in these, see the last one, across Stony Creek, before they are all gone and forgotten!

We followed the blazes to the gravel road through the nice woods of the area of Hopewell National Park and could see the vehicle in front of us along Route 345. We walked past the vehicle and did the tenth of a mile into the French Creek State Park lands to complete map 2 of the Horse-Shoe Trail.

We had been lost, then found. We saw a primitive stone working site, horses, blue birds, other hikers and the son of my high school chemistry teacher who I had never known to exist until our hike. We had completed another map, successfully crossed another cable bridge, enjoyed numerous sights, smells, and environments. We took a multitude of photographs and had some new insights on development of land. I had good company and enjoyed hearing their thoughts. Future hikes in the exploration of the Horse-Shoe Trail were another turnpike exit closer to home.

So ended day 12 on the Horse-Shoe Trail. It was a great hike!

Chapter 14

Five Young Women!
(HST Map 3, May 30, 1999.)

The hike on May 30, 1999, was from the vehicle parked along Route 345 at French Creek State Park to Alleghenyville Road, just past Maple Grove Speedway. Today's hike was of the park, hike and hope style of access and pick up.

Memorial Day weekend was obviously a busy day in French Creek State Park. All of the camp sites were occupied and many campfires were still smoking from last evening, or perhaps from rekindling this morning. The air was heavy with wood smoke; it wasn't choking, but definitely gave the impression of a large encampment.

Jeep Cherokees, Toyota Fore Runners and tents of every description and color were set up beside every tree. It was just like the orange hunting jackets beside every tree on the first day of deer season but the colors were different.

I had the need to use the rest room and detoured to a facility near one of the camping areas. About 100 yards from the "facility" I could smell it. At 50 feet, the aroma was so strong that it could stop a falling star. I decided to take my chances in the woods and returned to the trail.

French Creek State Park is a very scenic area. There was a fisherman on Hopewell Lake which was very quiet. A mist was rising from the surface of the water. We waved to each other through the rising mist but did not break the silence. Some carp were feeding very close to the shore and I attempted to photograph them, then continued on my way. (Photograph 42)

The dam at Hopewell Lake was a very interesting structure. It is stone and descends from the overflow at the top in a series of steps. I enjoyed some time admiring the design and construction of this dam and the area near the foot bridge across French Creek. (Photograph 43) As I neared the end of French Creek State Park, a runner was also entering the woods onto the HST from the park road. The air at this point now choked me with wood smoke from the nearby French Creek camp sites. I stopped and waved the runner through. "You're moving faster than I am, please go ahead."

"Thank you." The runner stopped. "Are you hiking the Horse-Shoe Trail?"

"Yes, I'm trying to reach Alleghennyville Road."

"There is a running race for Special Olympics which is going to follow the trail for about 20 Kilometers. It should start from the main park area about 10:00 AM. You may want to watch for them since there are about 250 entrants."

"Thanks for telling me," I responded. "I'll try to make the road before they overtake me."

"I'll probably see you later then because my wife and I are going to compete. I'm going to run the Sixpenny trail then go and get ready for the 20 Km run."

"Good luck and thanks for telling me about this so I can stay out of the way. I'll look for you later. Give me a shout when you go past."

I took out the trail guide and saw that I was at about mile 6 and needed to be just beyond mile 14.4 before the runners overtook me about 11:15, if I wasn't going to be an obstacle or need to move from the trail. I picked up my pace.

There is a thriving population of squirrels and chipmunks in the area of French Creek Park and they chattered, scolded and stared as I walked through their dominion. I tried to get photographs but they kept a good distance, or stayed on the back sides of the trees with just their faces peering around the tree. I tossed a stick beyond the tree where one squirrel had sought refuge to see if it would come to my side of the tree for a photo when the stick hit the leaves behind it. It worked. The squirrel did come to my side of the tree, but upon seeing me fled so quickly that I could not take a photograph.

As I passed the junction with Sixpenny Trail, I heard brush cracking just to my right and thought I had startled a deer. There was more noise in the brush but no snorting or pounding of hoofs. The noise was coming toward me rather than going away! Three bicycle riders appeared, riding through the woods. We exchanged good mornings and continued our respective ways.

Song birds of several species sang their songs in competition along this section of trail. A benefit of the coming runners was that the trail was very well marked since the Special Olympics event organizers had strung red ribbons and put white powder on the ground forming directional arrows for each turn.

The brush rattled in front of me! Bicycles? A flagging white tail in the underbrush told me that this time it actually was a deer.

As I crossed Geigertown - Birdsboro Road into the South Birdsboro Archery and Gun Club grounds I observed a man directing traffic into the parking area. I approached him and inquired if he were a member of this club. He was.

"Please pass on my appreciation for letting this trail cross your club grounds," I requested.

"You're talking to the right person, I'm president of the club."

"Well thanks. It's very nice for you to make a corridor for people to use the trail." I introduced myself and described how much I was enjoying the experience.

"Actually some of our members have a hard time with that trail. They worry that we're going to shoot somebody if they stray onto the ranges. I keep telling them that hikers and horseback riders are outdoors people too. We have to work together because God knows there aren't too many outdoors people left and we all have to work with each other or none of us will be able to go anywhere. The developers don't want anyone else on their property and some of our members are talking that way too."

I left the gentleman with my appreciation and a request to pass this on to the members. He indicated that he would do so.

Leaving the gun club I passed between the archery and rifle ranges. There was no hazard so long as people using the trail stayed within the designated corridor. It is kind for the members of the club to accommodate the other outdoors people who use the corridor they provide.

If you use the trail, please respect the privilege of crossing the property of our hosts. For your safety, please stay on the marked trail, especially in this area.

At the top of the first slight ridge, behind the ranges of the South Birdsboro Archery and Gun Club, I encountered what were commonly called deer flies in Weinel's Crossroads, Pennsylvania, where I grew up. This insect causes actual pain when it bites!

Unlike other flying insects along many trails, you can't miss this one when it is on the attack. It is like a supersonic fighter jet buzzing your head. I felt like Godzilla with the attacking airplanes buzzing my head. The insect flashed in front of my eyes, then I heard it buzzing past. I couldn't swat it because it was moving too fast. For the next two tenths of a mile I tried to swat this critter with my sweat towel without success.

Some trail stories I have read describe a particular insect as a "Can't see um." I decided to rename the deer fly "Can't miss ems!"

Looking for the view of new homes described in the trail guide at mile 9.1, I saw only the very tops of two roofs over the trees. There was little visible sign of a new development from this point on the trail. Nature does change landscapes with time!

The "Can't miss em" landed on my forehead, I swatted and enjoyed the feeling and sound of its exoskeleton being crushed between the back of my hand and my forehead. There was no pain. I got it before it bit me and didn't even break my glasses. It was a proud moment!

As I stood there with a smile of good riddance on my face and wiped the remains of the "can't miss em" on my sweat towel, a dog moved into view around a turn in the trail then came to an immediate stop and point. No barking, no movement! It was a beautiful dog, light chestnut brown with brown eyes, short hair and slightly smaller than a greyhound. "Good morning dog," I said. The dog's tail twitched, almost imperceptibly. It wanted to greet me but was trained not to move. Four hikers came into view moving toward French Creek State Park at a very respectable pace. We exchanged good mornings. The man in the lead spoke to the dog and it moved on by.

I told the hikers that they were the first people I had seen on the trail this day other than the runner. They reminded me that I would see hundreds of people later. I had no idea at the time, but I would also see all four of them again later.

Reaching the valley at mile 9.6, in the trail guide for map 3, I encountered a box turtle. It was inching along and was the first thing on the Horse Shoe Trail I saw moving slower than me. I stopped to take a picture to commemorate my passing of another hiker going the same direction, the first time this had happened in years! (Photograph 44)

Unlike the squirrels and chipmunks, The turtle was posing for the close up picture. Very photogenic and a natural model, it didn't even close its shell!

On the moist ground at the very bottom of the valley were two white moths which, at first glance, appeared to be Native American, flint, projectile points imbedded in the mud. I stopped and looked closely before it was apparent that they were moths and not flint artifacts. I made the assumption that the moths were extracting moisture from the damp soil at the bottom of the valley and moved on.

It was getting warmer. The temperature was in the mid- eighties, with the promise of a hot day. I was moving at a faster pace than normal as I hiked up the rise to the view of St. Paul's church in Geigertown and started perspiring profusely. The view of the church rising above the surrounding trees is inspiring. The trees are remaining around the church and frame it in a delightful way.

The symbolic religious aspect was also inspiring. I took two pictures of this view from different angles but a telephoto lens would have been very appropriate. (Photograph 45) Moving back into the woods, mountain laurel was blooming. The fragrance and sight of the blossoms was refreshing. (Photograph 46)

Leaving the woods I came upon a farm lane along a wheat field. This was a beautiful sight. (Photograph 47) Stopping here for a moment to indulge in the view of the field, the area was thoroughly appreciated and reminded me of my youth.

After a drink of water and a short walk, I arrived at an abandoned railroad bed and crossed an ancient iron bridge. I checked the compass direction from just beyond the bridge and discovered to my amazement that north was toward the bridge. This couldn't be?

I moved to the side and observed that the compass needle remained pointing to the bridge. Realizing that the iron in the bridge was affecting the reading, I closed the compass and examined the bridge more carefully. "P&R 1881" was visible in the three cast iron corner posts which remained. This bridge was a relic of another age and it was very interesting to examine the design, construction, and materials which have survived more than a hundred years. (Photograph 48)

The bridge has a posted weight limit of two tons and appears very solid except for a damaged corner post on the north east side and one damaged filler plank on the northwest edge.

The village with the barking dogs, described in the trail guide, was just ahead. The dogs were still barking! I considered that the dogs must have impressed the authors of the trail guide to earn a special mention. I wondered if these dogs had been barking continually since the trail guide was written? Had they ever paused in their barking in the three years since?

Three of the dogs ran up to greet me and have their ears scratched. They were very friendly and would individually stop barking when their ears were being scratched or they were being petted, but as soon as I reached to pet another, the dog I stopped petting backed up and started barking while the next one got petted. I now understood why the "barking dogs" were mentioned in the trail guide.

A girl came outside and called the dogs into a building. They all followed her and ceased barking once inside.

Just ahead, at the crossing of Hay Creek, was a most refreshing sight. Two young women, and a special child who appeared to have Down's Syndrome, apparently in the care of the two young women, had a table set up. About a hundred paper cups were set out upon the table which was covered with a neat and fresh table cloth. The cups were full of cold beverages and condensation had formed on the sides of the cups. There were also snacks arranged neatly on the table and as I approached I saw that the young women had about ten plastic gallon bottles of beverages cooling in the creek. These were tied to a tree with cord. Obviously, this was a support stop for the runners in the 20 Km run and it was well managed!

"Would you like some water or gatorade?" one of the young women asked cheerfully.

"I'm not one of the runners," I informed her.

"Oh, that's ok. We have enough for everyone. Please help yourself. We also have some cookie snacks. Here," she handed me a small cup full of miniature chocolate chip cookies which I gratefully accepted.

"Thank you. How soon do you expect the runners?"

"They got started a little late, so they're probably about half an hour away."

"Have you ever walked this trail?"

"No, we're just here to provide refreshments for the runners, then we're going to the pool at Sleepy Hollow for the awards ceremony and then to swim. Where does this trail go?"

"The trail goes from Valley Forge to the Appalachian Trail north of Harrisburg. I walked that part and now I'm walking from Valley Forge to Hershey a few miles at a time."

"That's a long way."

I explained about how a family trip had experienced a change of plans, why I had decided to complete the HST, and how interesting it was. We chatted for a few moments about my daughter and what a strong hiker she was. I told them about how frustrated Renee had been waiting for me on our hikes, not having a hot shower, and the fact that there were no "rewards" in the views from the top of the mountains we climbed, due to the forest canopy which covered everything. I shared how much I enjoyed being with her and the others on other hikes. I encouraged them to walk the Horse-Shoe Trail areas close to their home with their families or friends and described the nearby view of St Paul's Church. It was a nice break.

Thanking the young ladies for their hospitality again, I moved on to clear the narrow section of the trail before the runners arrived.

As I left this site, I thought about how nice it was to be so well treated and what living in a community where people were this courteous must be like. I was touched by the charm and hospitality of these young women and formed a positive impression of their families and community in the very brief time I had talked with them. They were like our neighbors.

The HST, at mile 11.6 of map 3, is a "long climb," as described in the guide book. It is also relatively steep in some areas. One of the signs for the runners said: "Do something dangerous." Running up this portion of the trail would definitely qualify. I wasn't being dangerous, I just walked.

At mile 13.1 I met a Scout Leader, with Scout Troop 543 of Hawk Mountain. I chatted with him as I caught my breath and mentioned that I had been in the Scout Troop of Allegheny Township, Westmoreland County, PA, as a youth. As I took my leave, he told me to say hello to scouts a little further up the trail. They were directing the runners at points where the race route changed direction from the HST. I saw the scouts and said hello. I asked if they were giving out Gatorade and cookies, but they weren't. I told them the young ladies at Hay Creek gave me some chocolate chip cookies but I ate them all. Some hard candy was offered so they wouldn't feel totally left out, but it was declined.

Major erosion of the Horse-Shoe Trail was observed in this area. The same type of erosion as in other areas where the trail vertically ascends a hillside, without drainage diversions, and the water runs down the active area of the trail corridor scouring all loose soil from the trail. (Photograph 49)

Checking the map again, I detoured north through the woods to Buck Hollow Road from about mile 13.8 to clear the trail for the runners. I didn't hold up any runners. When I reached Buck Hollow Road, the runners were already coming down the development road to turn left and up the slope on Buck Hollow Road toward Route 10, just west. The detour had been very prudent.

The first ten or so runners, including the women, were running strong and did not even show major perspiration stains on their shirts! They must be in really great physical condition I thought, continually wiping sweat from my face as I worked up the grade.

Every one of the leading runners who passed said "morning" or a similar greeting, as they ran up the road. The rapid "pit, pit, pit" sounds of their shoes on the asphalt announced their presence behind me and I moved onto the shoulder of the road to let them pass.

As I progressed up the grade, the rapid "pit, pit, pit" sound of the foot falls of the overtaking runners gradually changed to a less rapid "slap,..slap,..slap" sound. Now the shirts of the passing runners were drenched in sweat and they were struggling to maintain the rhythm of their breathing. The "good mornings" of the earlier runners now became gasps, or merely nods, as these more mortal beings labored up the increasingly steep grade, still at a run.

It was 11:30 AM and I needed to call Diane, my lovely bride, to tell her that I was going to go on to the second pick up point on Alleghenyville Road. This would be another two and one half miles, making the total 21.5 miles for the day, a very ambitious distance for me, but I was making good time and we had made contingency plans for alternate pick up points the evening before. We agreed that I would call before noon and announce my final objective.

A man was working in his yard and encouraging the runners coming past: "Only 500 yards to the top!" He informed the struggling runners as they came past.

"Is there a pay phone close?" I asked.

"No, but you can use my phone," he offered.

I gratefully accepted this offer and introduced myself. I called home on the credit card and placed a message for Diane informing her that I would meet her where the HST crosses Alleghenyville Road at 2:30 PM. Six miles in three hours should be no big deal and I had my lunch staged at Route 10. It was a beautiful day: go for it!

Thanking the gentleman for the use of the his phone, I walked outside with him. He informed me that he was retiring in eight days. We discussed the HST and how it used to run along the top of the ridge behind his home. He also pointed out the spring that was the origin of Hay Creek. I wished him well and continued up the hill. "Only 500 yards to the top", I heard him encouraging the runners coming up the hill, "would you like some water?"

At the top of the Buck Hollow hill, also encouraging the runners, was the runner I had spoken to at French Creek and his parents. They were watching for his wife and her friends. I crossed Route 10, retrieved my lunch and additional water bottles, then returned and talked with the folks waiting while I had lunch. The runner shouted a greeting as he saw his wife and her friends struggling up the hill. They were the same hikers I had seen going the other way, toward French Creek Park, earlier in the day. We exchanged greetings again.

The lady handed them each some of the cold water she had brought along, until it was gone. Another runner stopped and asked: "is this a water stop!" Her face was all red and her water bottle was empty.

"I have water," I offered, handing her one of the bottles which I had staged for lunch and resupply very early that morning and would not now be needing so badly because of the hospitality of the young ladies at Hay Creek. "Drink it slowly because it's very cold," I warned. I had frozen the spare bottles the night before.

"Oh, thank you," she said then continued on. The hospitality of the people of this area was contagious.

Talking with them, I learned that the dog which so impressed me was a breed from Czechoslovakia. I cannot pronounce it or spell it, but it was a very nice and well behaved dog.

Another item I appreciated were the police who were stopping traffic to let the runners cross Route 10. (Photograph 50) This is a very busy road and their efforts did much to contribute to the safety of the runners and the much slower hiker.

I continued on the paved road, sweating profusely. Presently I crossed Interstate Route 176 and came to another man directing runners onto the HST. We exchanged greetings. "There's a water stop at the end of the yard, get something to drink," he offered.

Thanking him I turned from the road and across the edge of the yard which descended gently into some woods. Just ahead were two more young women at a table and a young man, who appeared to be in their care, was to one side. All were lounging in folding chairs. "Good afternoon," I greeted them. There was no answer.

"Can I have a glass of water?" I asked. There were no cookies either.

"The water is only for the people registered in the race," one of the young women answered. I continued on by without breaking stride and wondered if these young women were from the same community as those at the first water stop about five miles before.

I reflected on family values and hospitality and realized what a positive impression the first two young women had made in just a few moments and, conversely, what a lousy impression the second two young women and the young man had made in even less time. I reflected on how we had trained our own children and hoped they would do better in a similar situation. I made a mental note to talk with our children to reinforce the expectation of basic hospitality even though they are adults and on their own because my initial and very positive impression of this community had just been cast into confusion and doubt.

Just beyond this point was the fifth young woman, picking up paper cups discarded by the runners. "Did you get some water?" She asked.

"I'm not in the race." I responded.

"Come with me and get some water," she insisted. "It's very hot and it's a long way to the next water." We walked back to the table where the water was staged and she handed me a cup of water which I gratefully accepted. This was confusing. The three people at the table never moved or spoke. Were they aliens?

I asked if this were her property and she informed me that it was. I thanked her for the water and for letting the HST cross her property. She indicated that she was always fascinated with the HST and would like to explore it further some day. I encouraged her to do that and took my leave.

Entering the woods again I reflected on the people I had encountered so far that day. Of the approximately 270 people encountered, not counting those who appeared to be in the care of others, most had been courteous, eight had gone out of their way to extend hospitality or to offer information or assistance, and two had been oblivious. I was disappointed in two but wrote them off as an anomaly because they just did not reflect the overwhelming positive experience in this area. I hope someone in this community helps to teach the second group of youngsters basic social skills and about hospitality. It is difficult to believe these young adults all lived in the same community.

Chapter
15

Lost, Confused and Frustrated.

(HST Map 3, May 30, 1999. (Continued))

On May 30, 1999 more people were encountered actually using the Horse-Shoe Trail in the area from French Creek State Park to mile 16.5 on the Berks County Map (HST map 3) than were encountered using the other hundred miles of the Horse-Shoe Trail that I had hiked to this point combined. It was enjoyable to chat with several of these folks and there were lessons learned. The most serious lesson however lay ahead as I entered the woods again at mile 16.5 of Horse-Shoe Trail map 3, working toward my objective of reaching the intersection of Alleghenyville Road and the HST.

Entering the woods at mile 16.5 in Berks County, Pennsylvania, the temperature was 93 degrees fahrenheit, my canteen was full and I had two hours to reach my pick up point five miles further up the trail at the scheduled time of 2:30 PM. I was somewhat concerned with the heat because it slows my pace and increases water consumption. In spite of this, I was confident that I would be able to achieve 2.5 miles per hour over the terrain shown on the map.

The gravel road at mile 17.9 was now paved. No big deal, the blazes were visible and there was no traffic at all. Crossing the small brook, I followed the trail to a meadow on the right, which appeared to be mile 18.6 or so. The blazes had vanished at the end of the woods! There were Christmas trees, or pine trees, on the right and uphill. A jeep trail or farm lane crossed to the right. I followed the jeep trail, or farm road, for about 1/4 mile. There were no blazes. I took out my trusty compass. The map showed the trail to go northwest, then west, then due south, then west again.

I returned to the last blaze. I should be turning sharp left, according to the map. The book said sharp right. I compromised and went straight ahead, coming through some woods and into another patch of evergreens. It occured to me that I was lost and I became concerned with the time.

Aha! I stumbled onto a jeep trail or farm road. I turned right and followed the road for about 1/4 mile searching for a blaze. None were found. I followed the farm road around the periphery of the tree farm to the right and still found no blazes. There was a very nice view of pine trees which I photographed. (Photograph 51) If you see this view while hiking the Horse-Shoe Trail, you are lost!

I decided to attempt to find the trail by following the edge of the upper woods due south and watching for where the HST entered the woods on the narrow trail at mile 19.0; then, if not successful, to seek Gebhart School Road by setting a compass course due west. At the end of the pine trees, where the road ran through hardwoods on both sides, a metal arrow pointed to the HST on the right. I was found, but it had taken almost an hour to accomplish this. The markings were very poor or I had missed all of them! Perhaps they were covered by brush or vines growing on trees?

It was now 2:15 PM and I hoped that Diane would be late to pick me up because I had no communication with her. I was getting tired and hot and wanted to hurry to the pick up point. Desperately, I wanted to be there in the next 15 minutes, but just could not physically do this. I did the best I could, even used the gravel drive under the power line to avoid being lost and confused again. Arriving at the pick up point at 3:20 PM, I was almost an hour late and Diane was not there!

I fantasized as I hiked toward the pick up point that I would arrive at the pick up point several moments before she would. What wishful thinking!

After thirty two years of marriage, I knew I wasn't abandoned. Did the van break down in the heat? Did the answering machine fail and she not get the message to go to pick up point # 2? Was she waiting in Plowville? Was I at the wrong place? It was 4:00 PM, it was very hot and I was almost out of water. I needed to do something.

I walked from the trail toward a house to use the phone to call home for messages and to ask for some water. No one answered the door at the first house I walked to. I continued east toward Plowville and came to the township police station. I asked the officer on duty if there had been an inquiry. No. Would he inform my wife that I was walking toward Plowville if he saw her? He indicated he would relay the message - if he saw her. I described our vehicle for him, thanked him and departed. I filled my canteen, took a long drink, and continued east.

At one home near Maple Grove Speedway there were several men sitting under a shade tree in the front yard. One man was napping in a reclining chair. I stopped, explained my situation, and asked if I could use their phone. The people were most understanding. They woke up the man taking a nap and I felt badly about disturbing his rest. Explaining the request again, he agreed to let me use his phone without hesitation. I called home on the credit card and there was no answer and no message. Diane drove past as I hung up the phone! "There she is!" I exclaimed.

"Wave down that van," the man shouted to the other men under the tree. They jumped up and whistled and waved. Diane turned around and came back.

"That van has been driving back and forth past here all afternoon," one of the men informed me. "We gathered she was looking for something."

"I hope I'm it," I stated and thanked them all for their help.

When Diane arrived it was a happy reunion. She was under a lot of stress because her mother kept insisting I was down somewhere along the trail with a coronary. Diane's mother had also speculated that if it was not a heart attack, then I must have fallen from a cliff and broken my neck. For the past two hours Diane had been hearing this line of speculation and was becoming increasingly concerned and stressed out.

From my perspective, I was relieved that Diane was not with the vehicle, broken down along the road in the heat, as I had feared. It was a very stressful situation for both of us and we were both glad to find each other.

It turned out that the roads identified on the map as Alleghenyville and Maple Grove Roads were both known as Alleghenyville Road to the local folks. Diane had waited for me for about 40 minutes at one place where the trial crossed Alleghenyville Road on the map, then went to where Maple Grove Road crossed the HST on the map, then went to Plowville. Diane was repeating this circuit about each half hour. She had left the pick up point about five minutes before I got there, returned while I was probably in the police station, and was on the third circuit when we found each other with some help from the local people.

In the future there will be a reconnaissance of the actual pick up point with both parties. Only one point will be selected for the actual pick up in cases where the other party will not be hiking with the individual or group being picked up. There is just too much confusion and stress created for an enjoyable hike, or ride to pick up the hiker, under these circumstances.

I recorded the man's name and address whose rest I had disturbed to make a request to use his phone in order to send him a thank you note.

It had been a good day in many ways. Things worked out fairly well in spite of the stress from being lost, late and confused.

Things which substantially detracted from the day's enjoyment were being lost, and poor logistics on my part in planning the pick up point.

On the positive side, a lot of nice people were met, more than even I would have imagined. The scenery was great, the historic railroad bridge was fascinating. I had located Maple Grove Speedway, which I had never managed to find when I actually lived in Lancaster County from 1975 through 1978, and I had developed a deeper appreciation for Diane as well as having the benefit of taking a map and compass on hikes reinforced again.

We drove back to the starting point at French Creek and toured the Hopewell Furnace site. The actual furnace was closed, but we had visited this site before, Diane thought. I was under the impression that the site that we had visited was the Cornwall Furnace in Lebanon County and some confusion remains on this matter. In any event:

So ended day 13 on the Horse-Shoe Trail. It was a great hike! It was even greater to rendezvous with Diane after all the confusion!

Chapter 16

Tower City.

(HST Map 6, May 30, 1999, With Diane)
(Pumping Station Road to Penryn Park)

My objective of completing the Horse-Shoe Trail and earning the "End to End" rocker was almost within reach. At this point I needed to complete Map 4, about three miles on Map 5 (PA route 501 to Pumping Station Road in Lancaster County), and the section of Lebanon County, Map 6, between Pumping Station Road and Aspen Road. Because of my enthusiasm, Diane agreed to go with me to hike part of the remaining trail in Lebanon County.

Looking at us with sad eyes that convinced us to change our minds, our dog did her best to make us feel guilty about leaving her at home. She succeeded. We got the leash and took the dog along.

The plan for this day was to take two vehicles, leave one at Penryn Park, and the other at Pumping Station Road. This would leave another evening hike of about four and one half miles to complete Lebanon County, Map 6. We called Penryn Park and left information about the vehicle, as requested in the Horse-Shoe Trail guide book, then departed for our hike. The gate at Penryn Park was closed so we parked one vehicle along the access road and drove to Pumping Station Road.

Tens of people were at the Pumping Station Road access area this nice Sunday afternoon. Several people were walking along Hammer Creek on the road, others were on bicycles, and some were just standing around talking. Taking our water bottles and "Shelby" we crossed PA Route 322 and followed the yellow blazes past the pink blaze at the start of the Conestoga Trail. We struggled up a very steep hill and onto a nice, rolling woodland trail across the top of the ridge through the state game lands.

"Shelby", was panting and her tongue was hanging out while we took a drink of water. We had not considered how she was going to have a drink from the canteen, assuming that she could drink from a creek or something. There were no creeks at the top of this ridge. I cupped my hands and Diane poured some water into them. The dog lapped at this gratefully, but more water spilled than was consumed by the dog. This technique was not working well.

Walking along the top of the ridge, we saw some bicycles going through the woods. Further along, we noted that trees were intentionally felled across some of the side trails. I wondered why someone would do this. Seeing what appeared to be sprocket markings on the tops of some of the trees which were across the one side trail, I speculated that the trees may have been felled to keep bicycles out of the game lands, away from the main trail. Judging from the number of sprocket marks, this did not work any better than cupping my hand for the dog to drink water.

Horse-Shoe Trail intersected Fire Tower Road at a "hairpin" turn, just as described in the trail guide. It was a tree lined asphalt road with good pavement and no cars at all! I did not remember seeing anything other than a driveway with a very elaborate gate as we passed the area from Penryn Park to Pumping Station Road. I asked a man who we saw where the road came out. "Did you see the big gate?"

"Yes?"

"This road comes out right below the big gate."

"I didn't notice it."

"It's not very obvious, but it's there."

"Thank you," I said, and we started up the side of the ridge. There was a good assortment of litter along this road, as with most roads, and I decided to recycle a discarded aluminum can into a drinking dish for the dog. Diane objected: "She will cut her tongue on that! Find something else."

Following instructions, I found a discarded styrofoam cup and cut the bottom off. The dog, and Diane, was pleased with this and "Shelby" happily lapped water from the cup. Continuing up the road, we could now see the towers. A lot of towers. There was the fire tower, now closed, and there were numerous other towers of every shape and configuration. Passing the trees on the opposite side of the road from the first group of towers, there was another cluster of towers. "Tower Space for Rent" read a sign on the side of a fenced area which was well populated. It was a city of towers and more were moving in. I wondered if the town of Tower City on Interstate Route 81, north of Interstate 78, had been named for similar towers.

Thinking of my cellular phone, that convenient device which makes mobile communication so easy, I felt a stab of guilt. Realizing that this city of towers is only one of the multitude of such sites which are the physical manifestation of the price for my convenience was somewhat of a reality check. How many more towers and tower cities are coming? Will each ridge have a future tower city to accommodate all of the newcomers. Are satellites better, or in 50 years will abandoned satellites cause the same problems for the next generation as the current generation has encountered with mine drainage? I questioned the price being paid for my convenience, but decided not to abandon this jewel of technology quite yet. On the other hand, I do not want to contribute to future environmental problems.

Past "Tower City" and back into the woods, we found the trail register and signed in. "Attempting to complete Lebanon County," I wrote.

Continuing to Penryn Park and detouring north of the ball field, we reached the pick up vehicle and returned for the second vehicle. It was nearing dark and ours was the only vehicle left in the Pumping Station Road parking area. With our departure, the woods grew quiet for another day.

Today I observed that off road bicycles may be a concern in state game lands and had witnessed an area where the possible destruction of healthy trees to prevent erosion and wildlife habitat destruction by bicycles had been carried out. I came face to face with one aspect of the price paid for my convenient cellular phone at Tower City. I had obtained an insight into how the name of the town of Tower City, north of the Pine Grove exit on Interstate Highway 81, just above the I 81 and I 78 junction at the top of another ridge, was probably named. We learned to take a device for the dog to have water from when on a walk in areas where there is no litter, which is anywhere away from roads, and we learned where Fire Tower Road intersects Route 322. I enjoyed Diane's company and was a few miles closer to my objective.

So ended day 14 on the Horse-Shoe Trail. It was a great hike!

Chapter 17

The Fox on the Fence!
(HST Map 4, June 5, 1999.)
(Alleghenyville Road to Mohns Hill Road)

Learning from the stressful experience of the park, hike and hope event, and bearing a large Hershey Chocolate Bar, with almonds, and a thank you note, I departed Saturday morning, June 5, 1999, for the Horse-Shoe Trail at its intersection with Alleghenyville Road. The plan for today was to do a shorter hike, but with new logistics because I was home alone. The first stop was the home of the man whose rest I had interrupted the week before to use his telephone.

Tokens of my appreciation, the Hershey Bar and the thank you note, were prepared to present to my host. Next, I was going to find a secure location to park my bicycle, which was in the vehicle. After finding a secure location to park the bicycle, the plan was to next locate a parking area for the vehicle near the Horse-Shoe Trail crossing of Mohns Hill Road. After parking the vehicle, I planned to bike to the bicycle parking spot, hike to the vehicle, then return for the bicycle. It sounds convoluted but it should work out.

I returned to the home where the "lost, confused and frustrating" hike had reached a happy conclusion last week and presented the man with the thank you note, the Hershey chocolate, and verbal expressions of my appreciation for his assistance. We talked about the Horse-Shoe Trail, about how nice it was to walk this trail and the sights along the way. We talked about employment, the Maple Grove Speedway, and where I could stash the bicycle. He offered to let me park it there, when I returned, and I accepted this offer gratefully.

Driving to Mohns Hill Road, I stashed two frozen bottles of water where the Horse-Shoe Trail intersects Witmer Road to assure that I would not run out of water if the plans fell apart, like they had last week.

On Mohn's Hill Road, there was absolutely no place to park. On the third drive by, I saw a man in his yard, stopped and asked him about a place to park. "Park here," he said. "The vehicle will be safe and its no bother." Thanking him, I secured my gear belt and hiking shoes to the bicycle and coasted down the steep grade into Adamstown, using the brakes the entire way. I was glad that I would not climbing this hill on the way back! Or would I?

On a downhill stretch, just before the spot I was going to park the bicycle, I saw a Pack and Play portable play pen at a garage sale. I stopped and bought this so that Diane and I would have a secure place for our grandson to play when he visited, then placed my purchase onto the handle bars of the bicycle and peddled to the home of the man who was letting me park the bike on his property. I told him I was back, changed shoes, stashed the play pen, changed into hiking gear, then set off for the Horse-Shoe Trail.

I reached the top of the ridge. Crossing under the power line on Alleghenyville Road, I thought about the logistics of last week's hike and about how this scenario was working out. I much preferred the logistics of the two vehicle system, used at Valley Forge, to the current bike and hike scenario. The bike and hike system was probably going to be better than the park, hike and hope system, tried last week, but it was a lot more exercise than I wanted since my objective was to hike the Horse-Shoe Trail. Another disadvantage to the bike and hike system was the fact that a relatively new bicycle is more likely not to remain where it is left than an old, worn out vehicle, or a new vehicle with a sophisticated security system. For this reason, the bicycle was left in an area which should be safe, about a mile from the start of the day's hiking.

I was captivated by the scene of a field of new corn where the Horse-Shoe Trail went west from Alleghenyville Road. The young, light green, corn plants contrasted vividly against the rich, damp, brown soil. The symetry of the rows of corn which were planted in curving rows, following the slope of the field and skirting the boundary of the woods, directed my eyes around the field like a skillful advertisment. The pleasure of the contrasting areas of light and shadow, bounded by woods and the contour of the land, the rich fragrances of the damp earth, the new corn, and the woodlands, could not be recorded with a photograph. Imagine the rich variety of fragrance as you look at the photograph of the area. (Photograph 52)

Care was taken to package the foil wrapping and cardboard from the camera in my gear pouch. Upon reaching the vehicle, the cardboard packaging was there, but the foil wrapper had been dropped somewhere. I am embarrassed that this happened. With this event, I had lost fully one half of the total pieces of litter (two) that I had found on the entire length of the Horse-Shoe Trail away from access roads. I do apologize for this. From this experience I now understand that some of the litter I found may have been inadvertently dropped, rather than intentionally thrown away. More personal understanding and support for the need to pick up and pack out the litter from others resulted from this event.

Hiking a nice trail through dense woods, I came to a tent near the clearing for the power lines. Calling hello and hearing no answer, I continued on my way. There didn't appear to be anyone there and I was somewhat surprised to see a tent in the woods with nobody around since there were no fishing spots or swimming areas near by.

Another small stream was observed and crossed. There were small minnows darting between the shelter of different rocks in the pools of water in this creek. Some erosion of the trail bed was evident in the area where the soil of the creek bed had been packed down by horses but it is a very pretty area.

Crossing the power line at mile 25.65 I sought the trail register at the top of the clearing. I didn't find it. I didn't find any more blazes either. In the woods at the far side of the power line, a blaze was found. Just beyond that was the trail register, in the dense woods. I was delighted to find the register since I had already missed one in Dauphin County due to a trail relocation.

Signing the trail register, I enjoyed reading entries from previous hikers and riders. Entries in this register were mostly from horseback riders. A box turtle shell was found on the ground nearby. After replacing the register, the shell from the box turtle was placed on top of the box then I continued on my way. After several more blazes, the trail vanished again!

Wishing I remembered where I had put the trail relocation information I had cut out from the back copies of the "Blaze," I searched in a widening pattern from the last blaze with no success. A complete description of the relocations of the Horse-Shoe Trail in the past year were in these articles. I had saved them so well that I couldn't find them myself!

I continued to descend, reaching the tributary to Little Muddy Creek described in the trail guide. I knew that a gravel lane went into the woods for some distance from Witmer Road since I had stashed my frozen water along this gravel road earlier in the day by backing the vehicle into the gravel lane. Also, I knew the road was close because the valley was narrow in this area.

Twice, in increasing distances, I walked along the bank of the creek looking for the foot bridge to cross the creek. No blazes, no foot bridge, and no gravel lane were found. Abandoning the search for a blaze, in frustration, I crossed the creek and came out of the woods and trees into the yard of a residence. Walking along the edge of the yard, I came to Witmer Road. About 200 yards away was a satellite dish which I recognized from earlier in the day. Turning right on Witmer Road I came to the HST crossing, indicated by yellow arrows on the road surface. Searching for another blaze in the area I had come from, I went down the gravel road to retrieve my water. A culvert had been removed from the gravel road. Was it the foot bridge? There were no blazes here either.

Eureka! I found it. The stashed ice had melted and was now very cold water. It was just where I had left it. It was great to have some cold water! It would have been excellent also to have found some trail blazes, but these were not found until I crossed the road and started the steep ascent to the top of the next ridge. Surprisingly this area was clearly marked and the trail was easy to follow.

The voices of a man and woman screaming at each other were clearly heard from one of the houses somewhere below as I reached the top of the ridge north of Witmer Road. This was the only screaming heard on the entire Horse-Shoe Trail. Gratefully, I was soon out of range of the loud voices as I crested the ridge and moved away.

The fine view of Adamstown from the power line described in the trail guide is obscured by trees and brush now. There was a view to the northwest but it was like looking out from a tunnel in some respects. The horizon was limited by the edges of the clearing. High weeds obscured any blazes in this area and I followed a narrow path to the bottom of the hill and PA Route 568. After crossing Route 568 there was no trail and there were no blazes. Once again, the trail appeared to end.

Reading the information in the trail guide, I noted that I should turn right along the woods. There were trees in a narrow strip at the bottom of the field and I returned to them. On the side of one of the trees, obscured by branches and brush, was a yellow metallic arrow, pointing into the trees. I followed the trees and came to a recognizable trail in about a tenth of a mile where a corduroy road, made from small logs placed side to side perpendicular to the route of the trail, crossed a swampy area. There were blazes here, to my relief, and I followed them to the crossings for the two creeks described in the trail guide. The trail emerged from the small woods onto a 90 degree turn on Route 568. It was a nasty corner for crossing the road, but probably the best spot available. I could now see a yellow blaze on a fence post across the road and, listening for vehicles, crossed.

A farmer was pulling a wagon of hay toward me, with a pick up truck, as I walked down the driveway toward the farm house. I waved as he came up the driveway and he stopped and chatted for a few moments. I thanked him for letting the HST cross the farm. He stated that he just rented acreage but would pass on my appreciation to the landowner. I walked around the house, petted the dog which came out to announce my presence, and continued on the lane that crossed Little Muddy Creek on a bridge which was actually present and easy to find. The water in the creek was very clear this day and it was a pretty area.

Crossing Route 222 was uneventful. Ascending the side of Adamstown Ridge provided some very nice views of the valley. The trail threads up a driveway, right beside a garage which has a blaze on it. It is really nice of the people along the trail to permit hikers or riders, to cross their driveways, lawns, and fields and to share the views of their lands.

An old logging road wound through new growth woods in this area with a creek on the down hill side. It was nice and I enjoyed this well marked and easy section of the trail after being "blaze less" so often in the past couple of miles.

Coming to, and crossing under, the power lines an old wire mesh fence was on my right, the down hill side. The mesh openings were about four or five inches square and the fence was about chest high. Ahead was an area where the fence was down, with the mesh leaning to the up hill side.

The rock fragments on this section of the trail were different than those I had seen and taken small specimens of so far on the Horse-Shoe Trail. It was an aggregate of stones embedded in other stones. The appearance of the stone was similar to very worn concrete on a roadway. Instead of the river gravel being exposed where the concrete had worn away, imagine that the river gravel had been replaced by round red stones. Near Valley Forge the stone was more of a gray limestone and white quartzite type. Later, the granite type of stone was prevalent. Here was a new type of stone and I realized that I was crossing a third manifestation of geological era or, mineral deposit, evidenced by the rock formations. Interesting. Picking up a specimen of this stone I continued up the ridge.

"YIP!" A single sharp and loud exclamation, similar to the bark of a surprised soprano dog whose tail had been stepped on, came from just in front of me. My attention quickly went from the stone I had been examining to the source of the noise.

Two red foxes leaped from the hay, or weeds, in the area under the downed fence post. One fox ran rapidly into the cover on the up hill side and disappeared with only a brief glimpse of its form and color. The second leapt away to the down hill side, crashing into the wire of the mesh fence, and being stopped. Recovering quickly, the second fox again attempted to leap over or through the fence. A second time it was forced back by the impact with the wire mesh. Recovering more slowly, or perhaps considering its options, the fox ran out from under the fence and through an opening, disappearing quickly into the cover and trees below.

This was the first time in years that I had seen a fox up close and personal and the only time in my lifetime that I had seen two foxes together. I was surprised that they were so close to the inhabited area I had just left.

Impressed that the two foxes had immediately split up and fled in different directions, I questioned whether this action was from instinct or strategy. The fact that the one sly fox had crashed into the fence twice before finding a way out of its dilemma, and into better cover, caught my attention. If the foxes hadn't yipped, but would have sat still or quietly slipped away, I probably would not have seen them at all.

The fox on the fence was a lesson in the element of surprise, which I had read about, reduced to a very succinct example: Even a creature "sly as a fox" makes dumb mistakes when surprised! Sometimes the same one twice.

The area was examined visually and audibly for evidence of a den under the fence. I did not approach the area the fox had been in for fear that I would disturb any young in the possible den site.

Happy to have seen the two foxes and to have had the element of surprise so well demonstrated, I continued up the trail taking the rock specimen along. The trail intersected a stone covered road in the woods, which was nicely shaded and featured a view of lawns and homes to the west. The sounds of children playing could be heard in the distance as I walked out to Mohn's Hill Road.

There were two scenic farm ponds along the trail here and this was a refreshing sight, especially with the temperature and the perspiration from the hike. I resisted the temptation to take a splash and continued to the vehicle. (Photograph 53)

Speaking with my host, I received permission to leave my bicycle there tomorrow at the start of my hike and to return for it later in the day. We discussed the Horse-Shoe Trail, employment, living in this area, and other topics. It was an interesting conversation and I thanked my host for the opportunity to use his property for a staging area.

Today I learned that I could drop litter without knowing, even though I tried not to. I learned about surprise. A new logistics system had been tested. I had met new, nice and interesting people. I saw two foxes and some new types of stone formations were walked over. I had been lost confused and frustrated, but found again and again.

So ended day 15 on the Horse-Shoe Trail. It was a great hike.

Chapter 18

A Wonderful, Mood Altering Fragrance
(HST Map 4, June 6, 1999.)
(Mohns Hill Road to Swamp Bridge Road)

The plan for Sunday, June 6, 1999 was to stop at the Route 322 and Route 72 interchange in Lebanon County to take a panoramic photograph of the view from this location before traffic started, then to get some breakfast and proceed to locate a parking spot for the vehicle at the end of Horse-Shoe Trail Map 5. After parking the vehicle, I planned to bicycle to the home of my host of the day before, with a Hershey Chocolate Bar as a token of appreciation, leave the bike, then hike to the vehicle and return for the bicycle.

Now hiking in Lancaster County on the Horse-Shoe Trail, it was more convenient to take PA Route 241 to the parking areas for this segment than to take the Pennsylvania Turnpike. On the way to the hike for the day I stopped to photograph the interchange of Route 322 with Route 72 and the surrounding area. Returning to PA Route 241, I stopped for a doughnut. "Hi Mike!" I heard a female voice ask "What are you doing out so early?"

I turned, somewhat surprised, and saw a lady that I knew from my job. "I was taking a photograph of the landscape from the 72/322 interchange and am now on my way to go for a hike."

"I would be interested in seeing the photos if they turn out."

Agreeing to share the photographs, I asked where she was going so early. We chatted briefly and I learned that she worked professionally with photography but right now needed to go to her "day job" at a local medical facility. She departed for work. I chose a doughnut and departed for the Horse-Shoe Trail.

Parking along Swamp Bridge Road, I bicycled north to Horse-Shoe Trail Road, southeast to Miller Road, south and east on Smokestown Road, turned north on PA Route 897, then, to my surprise, northeast on Mohns Hill Road. I was surprised because a road was indicated on the trail map but it was not named. It was like some of the other roads in this area - only the locals knew the name of the road, but not for certain unless they received their mail there.

The maps I carried were useful only to indicate that a road was actually present. The distance was about two and one half miles to where the road turned right to reach

Adamstown and the Horse-Shoe Trail. The bicycle needed an adjustment on the derailleur control arm because the chain was dragging on it in the higher gears and it would not down shift to the lowest range. I delayed the adjustment until I reached my destination.

The distance across this section of Mohns Hill Road was traveled in good order to the Berks County Line since the road followed the contour of the elevation so well that they appear as the same line on the map. The road was level. At the county line another surprise was in store. The road had been barricaded with large boulders and a large sign read: "Private Property." I checked the map again. The map clearly indicated that Mohns Hill Road continued through this point to the Adamstown Road section that I was on yesterday, intersecting in about 300 yards. The detour was six miles, per the map, including several miles on PA Route 272, a busy high speed highway. This was annoying!

Dismounting, I carried the bicycle over the barricade and walked it to the intersection of the other Mohns Hill Road on the still existing roadway.

Was this a land grab in progress? Did the Spring Township Supervisors sell or abandon the roadway indicated on the map or what? In any event, something is out of order here! The map needs updated, the barricade needs removed or both.

Winding down from the annoyance of the discrepancy between the map and the road, I entered the property of my host and greeted him with the Hershey Bar when he answered the door. We chatted for a few moments and he indicated where I should leave the bicycle. I changed shoes, removed and stored the bicycle safety helmet and took out the wrench to adjust the derailleur. Attempting to loosen the bolt which fastened the gear shift assembly to the frame, the head of the bolt snapped away before the bolt loosened and the derailleur fell off! I did not carry spare 10 mm bolts to secure this assembly and put the wrench away. I was truly grateful that I had waited to make this adjustment until I had reached my destination. This was one lesson that did not have a consequence of any great concern associated with it; I had planned to walk from here.

Removing the safety gear for the bicycle trip and leaning the bike against the shed, I crossed the yard to reach the Horse-Shoe Trail in the woods at the end of the lawn. I was pleased to be going back on the trail.

Winding through woods and up to the top of the ridge for about three fourths of a mile, I enjoyed this section. After cresting the ridge and starting down the western side, a deeply eroded section was encountered. As on previously deeply eroded sections, this was also on a steep vertical descent. There were numerous rocks along the eroded area and I constructed several steps in this section to reduce the force of water run off and reduce future erosion. After an hour or more of filling in the erosion gully with loose stone, I determined that I needed to be on my way. This job was more than one person could accomplish in an entire afternoon! Enough stones are lying loose on the surface of the land adjacent the eroded trail to fill the eroded area and also to form a french drain below the trail surface. I estimated that it would probably take ten or twelve workers two days to accomplish this repair, even with the materials at hand, and moved on to the farm below where several people and a happy puppy greeted me.

We, the people, chatted for a few moments. I thanked them for letting the trail come through their field and, with the dog in curious escort, continued to the "half way" sign for the Horse-Shoe Trail at the bottom of the field in the woods. (Photograph 54)

This sign brought a good feeling. It read:

"Stony Mountain 73.5" and "Valley Forge 59.6".

It was difficult for me to believe that I had walked almost 60 miles in the last month or so of weekends. Some with Michael and Ann, some alone, and some in the midst of a marathon race for Special Olympics. While this was the approximate mid point for hikers starting at either end of the Horse-Shoe Trail and walking through, I was nearing my objective of completing the trail since I had started in Hershey then hiked in both directions from there. Completed, to the west, were Dauphin County and more than half of Lebanon County. If things went as planned, I would complete Map 4 today, for a total of seven and one half of the nine maps completed. Although my bicycle was broken, Diane would be home tomorrow and the two vehicle system could be tried again, at an inspected pick up point.

Just beyond the half way marker was an electric distribution substation. I photographed this also because it brought memories of rewarding past work for the electric utility industry. (Photograph 55) Inexpensive and reliable power has improved the standard of living for most of us.

Reaching PA 897, again, there was a fragrance in the air that was very pleasant. I thought that it may have been coming from plants in the yard of the home beside the trail, close to where I was hiking, but could not be certain. I wondered what plant provided this overwhelming fragrance.

Walking the pavement along Smokestown Road, the temperature was increasing. The road was shaded ahead and a dog was speaking to me in terms that I could not understand from just inside the yard on the left side of the road as I walked past.

Reaching the shaded area, the fragrance that I had smelled shortly before was faintly present again. I looked for the source of this pleasant smell but could not locate it. As I walked, the smell became stronger. It was a nice fragrance, clean and invigorating. It was a fragrance so enjoyable that it must be illegal!

I enjoyed this wonderful, mood altering, fragrance for the next mile or so before determining where it came from. It came from trumpet shaped blossoms, some yellow and some white, on the same plant. I did not know what this plant was so photographs were taken of the plant in the hope that someone could help me to identify it later. From the photographs, I was informed that the plant with the great fragrance was honeysuckle. (Photograph 56)

The trail followed a wooden fence for a short distance, then led up a driveway to a farm. There were no markings here but the instruction in the trail guide to turn right at the Red Barn means hard right, not along the driveway, but to the edge of the woods to the right of the barn. I lost the trail and it took a few moments to figure this out. Not a frustrating or permanent lost, just a temporary lost.

At the Dutch Cousin Campsite, there are showers. The trail runs straight to the bottom of the road, past dozens of camp trailers, where it turns left 90 degrees. The HST then goes straight ahead, where the campsite road turns left again to return to the entrance, along a driveway. The Horse-Shoe Trail turns right from this driveway, follows a beautiful wooded corridor for about a mile, then vanishes just before the abandoned cabin described in the trail guide. The driveway for the cabin was found, the cabin was not. I watched for the sudden sharp right turn but did not see it. Perhaps the cabin and the trail markers were under the large tree downed across the trail in this area. The sound of traffic was followed to Reinholds Road and the Horse-Shoe Trail, which followed along the road in this area, intersecting Miller Road.

On Miller Road, in the numbers of the 560 series, what appeared to be raw sewerage was running from a pipe and draining into Little Cocalico Creek, about 150 feet below. This really brought home the point of why it isn't safe to drink the water from many "apparently" clean streams.

There were people riding horses in a field east of Ridge Road as I passed on the road. Shortly I reached the vehicle on Swamp Bridge Road. It was still there and the engine started. Good news! I was very concerned about the security of this parking area and decided to seek a better place to park the vehicle next week.

Driving back to retrieve my broken bicycle I reflected on the experiences of the day. Today I had learned that it is not good to attempt to make non-essential adjustments on a bicycle when you are far from home, far from a service facility, and far from your vehicle. The wisdom in the saying "If it ain't broke, don't fix it" was understood, even with it's inherent limitations.

It was learned that there is a serious discrepancy in the map concerning Mohns Hill Road in Berks County. I had met new, interesting, and helpful people.

Additional data on my trail erosion theory had been collected and some maintenance work had been done to reduce erosion. I had observed the halfway point on the Horse-Shoe Trail and had now been at both ends and in the middle.

Map 4 of the Horse-Shoe Trail had been completed.

So ended day 16 on the Horse-Shoe Trail. It was an invigorating hike!

Chapter 19

The Last Girl Scout Cookie!
(HST Map 5, June 6, 1999.)

After completing my hike for the day I had stopped to request permission to park the vehicle next week. The property was somewhat away from the Horse-Shoe Trail. A man answered my greeting and I spoke with him about parking the vehicle on his property the following week. He was interested in my hike.

"We used to take a week each year and ride the Horse-Shoe Trail, end to end. About ten of us would all ride together and it was a great time until they started displacing the trail onto highways."

"I noted about ten miles in Dauphin County where the trail is all on paved roads; and the area near the intersection of Swamp Bridge and Greenville Roads is probably one of the most dangerous sections I have been on because you can't get off the road in some areas close to there," I observed.

"Well, we rode the trail for the last time in 1990. My son's horse backed up into a truck where the Horse-Shoe Trail Crosses PA Route 422 in Palmdale, near Hershey."

"Was he hurt?"

"No, but the horse was injured and the truck was damaged. I can understand why some people don't want the trail coming through their yard, but I was really disappointed with the Girl Scouts."

"What did they do?"

"One day the Girl Scouts told the Horse-Shoe Trail to `Hit the Road,' literally! About 1990 or 1991, they just removed the trail markers from the camp and put the trail on the paved road, even though there was a right of way. The (HST) club met with them and were told the Scout Council just could not accept responsibility for the girls being exposed to trail users."

"The Girl Scouts is the organization that wants their members to have use of all the game lands and all the public property. They are the one organization who should understand the value of keeping a trail off the road, but when it comes to their property, everyone else should stay off! You're going that way. You' ll see what I mean."

"Where is the section you are referring to?" I asked.

"From Netzley Drive to State Game Lands number 46. You look at this when you walk past. There is no reason they can't allow a corridor beside the road. I knew one of the ladies on the Council. I used to be a big supporter of the Girl Scouts but I told her then that I would never support them or buy another Girl Scout Cookie again. That's ten years ago and I haven't bought a Girl Scout Cookie since!"

Chapter
20

Iron Icebergs!
(HST Map 5, June 13, 1999.)
(Greenville Road to PA Route 501)

The plan for today was to hike from Greenville Road to PA Route 501, using the park, hike and hope method. Diane and I had scouted the area in advance and Diane knew where the Horse-Shoe Trail crossed Route 501. There were no alternate pick up points!

The plan for the day also included stashing frozen water where Kleinfeltersville Road intersected the HST to assure that I would not run out of water. I carried my lunch, not wishing to find it eaten by wildlife in the area, and that most convenient device, the cellular phone.

After parking the vehicle I departed up the hill to the intersection of the Horse-Shoe Trail on Greenville Road and turned left along the edge of a yard, and a home, into a short area of woods. I looked forward to the tall trees described in the trail guide and followed the blazes. Instead of "tall trees" I soon found myself in a "clear cut!"

The trail had vanished! There were about a hundred acres of branches and tree tops. No tree bottoms, only stumps. No blazes, only an obstacle course. Starting to cross this area, I thought better of it. The branches were very deep and it was the best designed obstacle course I had ever encountered, even better than the ones from Basic Military Training three decades ago! This area was more difficult for walking than mountain laurel because the footing was so erratic. Each step onto a limb or branch was dangerous because all the branches were loose. With very dense brush, at least the roots are stable. Each step here had the risk of a fall where my legs and feet could be caught in branches and may be twisted or perhaps broken, before they came loose. Deciding that I should retreat before experiencing a disaster, I retreated to the edge of the clear cut and consulted the map in the trail guide again.

I photographed this most formidable obstacle for posterity. It is a remarkable engineering achievement that was not planned this way, but happened regardless. (Photograph 57)

To reach the trail from here I should have to climb about a hundred feet, in elevation, up the side of this hill, making the assumption that the elevation intervals on the map were at 20 foot increments. From the top of the hill, I would travel slightly south, followed by a turn to the west. After traveling west, about two tenths of a mile, I should intersect the road.

Climbing to the top of the ridge, I used the compass to set a course for Wallows Hill Road. Before reaching the road, I found the trail again.

Following the blazes of the Horse-Shoe Trail to and from woods, paths and various roads, the scenery in this area was more "appalachian" in character than any of the historic, urban, or rural areas traversed on the HST to date. This area reminded me of various areas in the Appalachian Mountain region where I had seen old cars, out buildings and farm equipment rotting in fields and could not comprehend why it was not taken to the scrap dealer and reprocessed. Perhaps the owners of the property let the materials sit here for fifty or more years and what did not rust or rot away became an antique? In any event, the character of much of this area was definitely different from that of the many other portions of the Horse-Shoe Trail and gave a very new, and somewhat surprising, dimension to the experience of hiking the trail.

At the sheep farm indicated on the trail guide, there are no more gates. The HST is routed at the bottom of the farm and there were no gates or sheep evident.

Shortly after the sheep farm, the trail travels for 2.3 miles on Netzley Drive, which also had a unique character. The homes along this stretch, which were visible from the road, were quite nice. It appeared that many of the people who own property along this road are very insecure, or security minded, based on the numerous security systems monitoring driveways and even the openings between trees along this road in some cases. I waved as I passed these homes in the event motion activated security cameras were recording my passage. I hoped the people were not that paranoid but I did want to be polite.

Passing a property with a stand of bamboo growing into the shoulder of the road, I wondered where the snow plows deposited their product when working to clear the street. I noted that the driveway was strategically placed at the end where the plow would come from, assuming the plow was working in the conventional direction of travel. I wondered if any plow jockeys ever caught the dickens from the property owner for plowing in the opposite direction when they did this section of road and leaving a huge pile of snow in front of the strategically placed driveway? I also wondered if the township ever had been assessed for damage to the dense crop of "ornamental" plants when plowing snow in the conventional direction? (Photograph 58)

Traffic was minimal here. It wasn't any wonder since vehicles probably had to be cleared in advance, or have a code transmitter device to leave the road without setting off security alarms. The feeling of these two miles was unfriendly and no one came out of their secure "compounds" to change this perception. Was it the neighbors?

Girl Scout Road had a lot of traffic. There was limited sight distance and the traffic moved along at a pace which did not consider that other vehicles or pedestrians may be present.

Hazards exist here because of the lack of a good shoulder on the road and obstacles just off the road. In the interest of personal safety, I remained diligent for approaching vehicles and moved from the road several times while hiking on the section of Girl Scout Road between Netzley Road and Furnace Hill Road to get out of the way of vehicles passing in opposite directions of travel. I clearly understood the concern of the gentleman I had spoken with the week before. A trail corridor off the road, even ten feet or so, as in the Valley Forge area, would make this area much safer for pedestrians, horse riders, and motor vehicle drivers alike.

Furnace Hill Road did not have the volume of traffic experienced on Girl Scout Road, but the same conditions were encountered. I can not understand why the Penn Laurel Girl Scout Council would displace the Horse-Shoe Trail literally onto the road when there was so much room to put a twenty foot corridor along the edge of the road and keep trail users safely out of traffic.

I was very disappointed to see that some of the elements of the story which I was told last week may have merit. I was even more disappointed that after ten or so years as a scout and with several decades of supporting scouting, to the extent of purchasing Girl Scout Cookies from every young Girl Scout that came to our door, that a scouting organization would have a major trail running on their property, displace the trail onto a highway, and not provide a corridor. In fact, I was amazed that the Girl Scout Council would not provide a corridor on their property to set a positive example of service to their youngsters!

Scouts are the national organization that promotes outdoor skills and activities, aren't they? Scouts are where I learned to canoe, where I went fishing on Mr. Weimer's farm and experienced my first sighting of a red fox, where the leaders confiscated my Hershey Bars at camp, where I learned to read a map and compass, all on private property used with permission.

Experience at my first visit to scout camp, where three bushel baskets full of candy were confiscated shortly after our arrival, even though no one admitted to having any candy, provided an understanding of the miracle of the loaves and fishes in the Bible. There was no candy permitted in Camp BuCoco. That was a rule! Yet, at the end of the first day's activity, three full baskets of candy were collected by the Scout Leaders. This was all taken from the packs of young Scouts who certainly would not dare to risk being sent home from Scout Camp for breaking the rules!

I remembered this event every time the miracle of the loaves and fishes was mentioned in church. For several years, I tried to understand the miracle of the Camp BuCoco candy bars. Eventually I did come to understand how this event came about, and perhaps the other one too.

Walking on the road, and looking at the "no trespassing" signs on the first row of trees, I remembered a Norman Rockwell Painting of two young, cherry skinned, cub or boy scouts (perhaps one of each) helping a smiling, bespectacled, elderly lady across the street. Can you imagine their feelings when her daughters told these young scouts: "Yo! Hit the road! And stay off our mother's property!"

With each step I took on Furnace Road, and each "no trespassing"sign I read, the question repeated in my mind: "What has happened to the Girl Scouts?" The demeanor of the young women selling their cookies is not reflected in the leadership of their regional camp site!

It also ocurred to me that perhaps highway and township road rights of way should be modified to include a corridor for pedestrian travel as the Pennsylvania Turnpike provides in an earlier section of the trail. It may not be a bad idea to consider mandating this practice for development of corridors in more urban areas either.

It was so refreshing to enter State Game Lands number 46 with mature trees, a nice trail, and a welcoming environment, that I stopped and relished this experience; thinking that perhaps I have had my "Last Girl Scout Cookie" also!

I photographed this area to remember how welcome it caused me to feel. It is very nice to have game lands both as a hunter, and just to go for a walk in the woods. Although I have not hunted in a state game lands since our son bagged his first squirrel, I made a mental note to continue to purchase a hunting license every year, whether I go hunting or not. I will be able to cover the cost with the savings from cookies!

With this happy thought, I continued descending to Klinefeltersville Road and Middle Creek at the discharge stream from the dam at the Middle Creek Wildlife Propagation Area. I sought out my water bottles and checked the tell tales for tampering. All was in order and a cold drink of water was a pleasant treat.

Crossing Middle Creek, I observed that the name was confused. This creek should be named Muddy Creek 2. The waters were polluted with feathers and excrement from the multitude of Canada Geese and other wildlife and were the color of mud. (Photograph 59) I crossed the road and sought out a stump or rock in the cool wooded area to pause for lunch.

Drinking the cool water, from the previously frozen water bottles, with lunch was also a pleasurable experience. As lunch was enjoyed, a deer snorted up the ridge and walked toward me. The deer saw me, snorted and bolted several leaps up the ridge. Taking out the camera, I hoped for another view of the graceful animal but it didn't come into view.

After packaging and storing the refuse from lunch inside the loop of the guard rail, to be picked up later, I continued up the hillside and saw the deer again. For the second time, I didn't get a good picture, but I did enjoy seeing the deer.

Walking up the ridge, my attention was drawn to a smooth, wet, reddish brown stone buried in the trail. I tried to pick the stone up but it was too firmly imbedded in the trail to pull out. Other stones around this stone were not wet, in fact there had been no rain for several weeks. Further up the ridge, other stones of the same color were found which were also wet! My curiosity was fully piqued. How did this stone get wet? Was it porous and conducting water from the ground? Examining the other stones which had water on them, I attempted to pick them up also. They were all firmly embedded in the trail. Scrapping away the material covering one of the stones with a stick and my knife, I found the answer to the moisture. The stone exposed on the surface of the trail was the tip of a large, ironstone deposit below the surface. An "iron iceberg!"

The exposed stone was much cooler than other stone on the trail. This may have been because the large stone below the surface was cold enough and had adequate heat transfer properties to remove the heat from the surface material faster than the surrounding air could warm the stone. In this manner, the cool stone condensed the moisture in the air on its surface, causing the wetness which I had noticed. This was a fascinating phenomenon. I found a loose piece of the stone, which was not moist as the attached stones, and kept it for a souvenir.

The trail here is very nice and very well constructed. The walking is easy and the sights, sounds, and smells of the forest make for a very enjoyable walk in this area. The fact that the "commanding view" to the north, described in the trail guide has been commandeered by the plant growth, is compensated for by the interesting plants and stone specimens in view along the route. In the winter season, the view to the north will probably be better because the close up view of the abundance of plant growth here will probably diminish with the first frost of the season.

Descending to Segloch Road, the yellow blazes just end. The trail continues to the north, but is "blazeless."

Just beyond the point where Segloch Road crosses clear and sparkling Segloch Run, a young man, Eric, was standing beside a burned out truck. Obviously, this had just happened.

"I have a cell phone if you need to call for help," I offered.

"My friend is already coming to pick me up," he responded.

"What happened?" I asked.

"The dog and I just left for a walk. We were just about 200 yards into the woods when I heard people screaming and hollering by my truck. We came back and the truck was all burned out. The dashboard was destroyed, the overhead fabric on the inside of the cab was totally burned, the seat was partially burned, and the insulation on most of the wiring was burned away. Some people riding horses saw it on fire and put it out with water from the creek."

"Do you have any idea what caused the fire?" I asked.

"I was getting a bottle of water from the truck and may have broken the tip of my cigarette off moving the seat. I believe the tip of the cigarette is what caused the fire."

We chatted for a few moments and I continued into the woods. The trail was covered with iron bearing rock and some very unique rock formations were in this area, including a stone "mushroom." (Photograph 60)

The trail in this area is an old carriage road. It is probably a hundred years old and is still in great shape. A little rusty, perhaps, but well constructed, drained and designed. Walking along Furnace Run on the carriage road is like walking into the past. The role of the Iron Furnace in this area is a large and interesting part of Pennsylvania and national heritage. The effect of the clear and pitcturesque creek along the carriage road, embraced by the forest, is special to experience. I stopped and enjoyed this area as I called for extraction.

"Hello? Hi, Honey. Can you come and pick me up?"

"I'll be there shortly."

I lingered for a while, enjoying this area, then walked up to Route 501 and sought out an area wide enough for Diane to see me, then safely pull off the road to pick me up to take me back to the staged refuse, the other vehicle and home.

Today I had learned that clear cuts are somewhat dangerous to walk through and are actually a formidable obstacle for foot traffic. This probably means they are good cover for wildlife.

I had experienced sections of an appalachian life style that were another dimension of this trail and reminiscent of other areas of the country; and an upscale, adjacent, area that actually felt unfriendly.

I felt very badly about the area of the Horse-Shoe Trail displaced onto the pavement at Girl Scout Road and wondered if this was the same road depicted on the cover of "Boy's Life" four decades ago.

I now felt very good about the fact that I purchase a hunting license and gained an appreciation for the value of the resource that State Game Lands provide to the public, even if I had been frustrated that there are so many hunters and so few obvious game animals in them when I go hunting.

Today I realized that game lands provide a very beautiful and welcome environment to hike through.

I was fascinated by the thermal conductivity of the iron bearing stone and the phenomenon of the moisture on the surface of the stones connected to iron deposits below.

I had enjoyed the deer and other wildlife and became concerned with the goose poop pollution in Middle Creek.

Today I had witnessed where some horseback riders had performed a good deed and where a dropped cigarette tip had caused a truck to be partially destroyed by fire.

I had committed to check into the situation with the Horse-Shoe Trail and the Girl Scout Council to see if the unsafe condition for the HST on Girl Scout Road can be reconciled.

Construction of the carriage road and the condition it is in today, had impressed me, even if it is rusty!

And, I had completed most of another map of the Horse-Shoe Trail, and exercised my mind and body.

So ended day 17 on the Horse Shoe Trail. It was a thought provoking, insightful and fascinating day as well as a great hike!

Chapter 21

Tick Infested!
(HST Maps 5 and 6, June 16, 1999.)
(PA Route 501 to Pumping Station Road)
and
(Penryn Park to Spring Hill Acres,)
(with Larry Taylor)

Vacation, my definition: "That period of time before which one attempts to complete all outstanding projects in order that after which unfinished projects left do not compete for limited time with the numerous projects, and the occasional crisis, which will always materialize during this period."

Hiking the Horse-Shoe Trail "End to End" was a project which I had taken on casually and now had only 2.2 miles of Map 5 and about four miles of Map 6 to complete. Completing the hike of the Horse-Shoe Trail was something I was going to accomplish before vacation, which started on June 19, 1999. I wasn't sure how this was going to be accomplished, but it was now a personal commitment.

Because I had not hiked through to Pumping Station Road on June 13, to complete Map 5, and because Diane and I had hiked a section of trail on May 30 which was not an extension of previously completed areas, I now had four "loose ends" of trail to connect, with about 4.6 miles of completed trail in between. This was poor planning, and removed options on how to complete this section in one day. Watch for loose ends if time is important to your hike.

I described my objective and plan to complete the Horse-Shoe Trail over the next two evenings to Larry Taylor, the staff engineer where I work. Larry is also a friend and Scout Leader who I had joined in camping and hiking with his scout troop from Shafferstown, Pennsylvania, on the Appalachian trail earlier in the year. Describing my logistical error and plans for completion over lunch, I asked if he would mind picking me up at Pumping Station Road, then dropping me off at PA Route 501 on his way home from work on Wednesday evening. Much to my surprise, Larry indicated that he would come with me to share in the completion of my Horse-Shoe Trail hiking project. I was delighted for the company and the help.

Leaving my vehicle at Pumping Station Road, we drove to CJ's Restaurant on PA Route 501. This was just a little over a quarter of a mile from where the Horse-Shoe Trail intersected PA Route 501.

Walking on the side of the highway, dodging traffic and struggling to keep our footing on the steep slope outside the guide rails, we reached the intersection of the Horse-Shoe Trail and started up the hill to the west. The trail soon came to a clearing for a gas or power line right-of-way which had a dirt trail. Following this trail we chatted about various work related subjects, falling into single file where the weeds and briars had choked out one track or the other. After a short descent back into the woods, there was a small sign which read: "CJ's Corral, Hikers Welcome." There was a directional arrow and a distance indicated. Wow! A Horse-Shoe Trail billboard!

CJ's billboard was the first advertisement that I had ever found on a hiking trail and I was impressed. It was small, neat, and unobtrusive. Thousands of images flashed through my mind of places from Maine to Missouri and Ontario to Ohio. Places observed in more than four million miles of highway, train and air travel. Of these thousands of images, not a single one said "Hikers" welcome. Was this a paradigm which caused tourists, truckers, pilots and others to only see the signs which welcomed them? I thought more carefully. No, I had not observed a "Hikers Welcome" sign before that I could remember.

"Isn't that the place where we parked?" I asked Larry, puzzled as to why we had worked so hard to get back to the Hosre-Shoe Trail from the parking area.

"Yeah." After a short pause he explained. "Well if I had told you the trail was right behind the restaurant then you wouldn't have hiked the Horse-Shoe Trail, you would have hiked MOST of the Horse-ShoeTrail," Larry offered with a smile. There was merit in his comment.

As the song said, we had a long way to go and a short time to get there. We continued up through the woods on a rocky but nice trail and I began to perspire profusely. Noting a crawling sensation just above the elastic on my sock, I reached down to scratch and found a tick. "I have a tick," I announced. Crushing the tick between fingernails, I examined my exposed skin for others and found two more. Removing these, we did a tick inspection of each other and found more ticks, which were removed and dispatched.

"We probably got these in the high weeds," I speculated. Larry agreed. None of the ticks had achieved a mandible lock on our skin. We continued to follow the yellow blazes of the Horse-Shoe Trail into the Camp Mack Boy Scout Reservation. The trails were very nice and well maintained here. I was pleased that these Scouts had the courtesy to let hikers cross their property and thought that this was more like the organization I remembered.

Eagle Rock is an interesting rock formation. "This trail," Larry explained, indicating a long, steep, but clear side trail, "is where we send the scouts for exercise when they have trouble going to sleep."

"Does it work?" I asked.

"Oh, Yeah! Sometimes it takes more times up and back, but it always works eventually!"

I understood this perfectly, remembering Airborne Training School at Fort Benning, Georgia. The state of Georgia probably still had not yet recovered it's original elevation after sinking from all the paratroopers in our training class doing push-ups by the hundreds. The saying was that with each push-up we did, Georgia sunk a little. "Builds character, does it?"

"That and gets everyone tired enough to go to sleep."

"Perhaps they become educated to be quiet so that you think they are asleep," I speculated. I then realized, with an insight, that some things just don't change. For the first time I understood the drill instructor's perspective of Airborne Training School discipline after more than three decades. It wasn't that you needed to be asleep, you just had to be quiet so that others could sleep. If you couldn't be quiet, you could be so tired after the exercise that you could then go to sleep. Quiet, among other things, was achieved in the end either by self discipline or by exercise to the point of exhaustion. Brilliant? Not really. Practical? Absolutely.

We continued to follow the yellow blazes. I smiled as I thought of Jump School. I could still remember the Drill Instructor's voice: "Drop and give me ten!" Push-ups were understood, and the entire group would drop and count out ten push-ups. After several events of being assigned push-ups for infractions of rules, with the rest of the training group doing the punishment together, an individual also received peer pressure to get his act together! We lost about half of our classmates to drop out, mostly from the exercise.

The Boy Scouts lose very few of their class mates since they have longer to learn their lessons. I wondered if everyone who completed jump school had been a Boy Scout?

The abandoned cabin at the power line, described in the trail guide, has collapsed. Remains of a gas stove and a gas powered refrigerator with ammonia coolant are scattered along the trail. The cabin is a hazard since the floor is not supported except in the corners, and the roof has fallen onto the floor. We stopped and examined the construction of this cabin for a few moments, mourned its collapse, then continued to Hammer Creek.

Bicyclists were crossing logs on the trail along Hammer Creek on Mountain Bikes. They pulled the front wheel up, leaned forward, and rocked the bike across the log on the front sprocket. They were impressive to watch. I didn't know a bicycle could stand this type of use and that riders could demonstrate this much control of the equipment. There was no damage to the trail from the bikes in this area since the trail was constructed in a manner that the bicycles didn't cause erosion or grooving. The obstacles the bike riders so appeared to enjoy were constructed in a manner that foot and horse traffic could easily negotiate. This was a good example of a multiple use trail which appeared to safely accomodate bikes, hikers and horses, without the trail and habitat damage seen in other areas along the HST.

The discipline of the bike riders to stay on the suitable trail area in this location and to construct their obstacles in a manner which others could easily avoid is commended. The courtesy of this group of bike riders, as we passed, was also a very welcome difference from what I expected.

Reaching the bridge across Hammer Creek at PA Route 322, I noted the Sullenberger monument on the north west side of the bridge. "Environmentalist" the plaque stated. I made a mental note to see what works were accomplished by Mr. Sullenberger and we went to the vehicle to drive to CJ's Restaurant to leap frog vehicles and complete the remaining section of my Horse-Shoe Trail "end to end" hiking project.

Parking my vehicle at Aspen Road, we returned to Penryn Park and parked Larry's vehicle just outside the now open road gate. Taking flashlights, in addition to the map, compass, snack, and water bottles, we struck off to intersect the Horse-Shoe Trail along the right field line of Babe Ruth Field.

"Babe Ruth played here" the sign read. We discussed whether it was THE Babe Ruth and concluded that it was more likely to be a "babe" named Ruth, who happened to be at the YWCA Camp, than the Babe Ruth of the baseball hall of fame. An interesting sign in any event.

Following the yellow blazes onto the power line roadway, we saw that this road, which the trail used, was constructed of slag. I wondered if the slag was a by product of the iron furnace which was located at Cornwall in years past, or if it was from a more recent period. From time to time a yellow blaze was found on a large rock along, or in, the road.

Reaching a swampy area in the road, we detoured through the brush to avoid walking through the boot deep water on the road. Coming out of the brush I felt insects crawling on my legs. Looking at the skin exposed below my hiking shorts, numerous ticks were obvious. "I have ticks," I announced to Larry.

He checked himself. "Me too," replied. We picked our respective ticks, then inspected each other for others and found several more. This place was infested with ticks!

Larry was better dressed to prevent ticks than I was. He wore a wide brimmed hat, long sleeved shirt and full length trousers which covered his boots. I wore hiking shorts which came to just above my knees, a short sleeved shirt, and my socks were rolled down at the top of my hiking boots. There were several ticks between my socks and ankles. Larry had one on the skin on the back of his neck. Both of us had several ticks on our clothing. We checked the time to make sure we had time to return home and do a thorough check for ticks under our clothes within three hours. Supposedly, it takes about three hours for a tick to bite, digest and infect a host with any disease it is carrying in its digestive system. If we didn't get lost, we still had plenty of time and I had "tick pliers" just in case.

I didn't want to get into equipment but "Tick Pliers" are a device which have a head designed to grasp the tick between its head and body without squeezing the body and injecting any fluids which may be presented during the removal process using a squeezing device. Tweezers, hemostats, forceps and most other mechanical clamp type devices have a much higher probability of actually injecting fluids into the skin of a tick host than a device which does not grasp the body. Use of fluids such as nail polish remover, are reported to cause the tick to inject fluids to remove its jaw parts from the skin of the host. Whether this is a sales gimmick or reality, it sounded good to me and I carried this device. Happily, none of the numerous ticks on my skin, or the one on Larry's neck, had imbedded their grappling mandibles into us and were merely loose on the surface of our skin. The ticks were easily removed without threat of infection. For this we were both grateful.

We continued to follow the yellow blazes through several more swampy areas, removing ticks each time we went through brush. Happily, the trail led into a wooded area with a wide clear path where the tick attack diminished.

In these woods at the top of a slight rise, Larry opened his convenient technological device, the cellular phone, and attempted to call home. The line was busy. We waited a few moments, performing an inspection for the smaller deer tick, then Larry tried the call again. Still busy.

Continuing on, enjoying the nice trail, the deep woods, and the absence of crawling creatures on our skin and clothing. Larry tried the call again about a mile later, still busy. "I swear, the internet is more difficult to keep the kids out of than the cookie jar ever was for my parents!" He said.

This amused me. I understood what he was saying. The internet has so much information and such diverse areas of opportunity that it has a lot of appeal. The level of internet appeal probably increases significantly when the kids are home alone.

We continued across a nice bridge that needed a few replacement planks and crossed back under the power line, checking for ticks again and finding several more. After removing the latest batch of ticks we crossed another small creek and came out of the woods along a developing area of Spring Hill Estates.

There was a blaze along a wood line and we followed a dirt and gravel lane that ran generally north. We came to a building which appeared to be a maintenance shed, but there were no yellow blazes. Beyond the building was a house. "At this point, if we can get to the road which accesses the house, I can tell from the map where we are," I said.

"Let's go back to that last blaze and go straight ahead, rather than crossing the yard," Larry suggested. We turned back and stopped at the last blaze. Looking at the trail guide we noted that it read: "when house ahead, turn right on gravel road." There was no gravel road, but there was a dirt path. The path ran in the right direction but it was supposed to be a gravel road. Any road will do in a well mapped development, I thought. We took the path, it was well used.

"I smell my vehicle," I teased.

"What does it smell like?"

"Burnt grease from all those miles."

"Yeah, right."

The dirt path was covered with gravel. A paved road was just ahead. Ash Lane. We turned right, the vehicle was in sight! The journey was complete.

"Congratulations," Larry said extending his hand.

"Thank you," I responded, shaking his hand, "and thank you for helping me to overcome the logistics problem."

"I enjoyed it."

"Me too. I'm actually excited about having completed the entire trail, but still don't believe I actually did this."

We got into the vehicle and went back to Penryn Park to Larry's vehicle. It was nearly dark when we left and this seemed symbolically appropriate for the last section of the hike. As we left the access road and turned in opposite directions, we waved goodbye.

Today I had seen the first sign I remember which welcomed Hikers! We had been infested with ticks and removed them without needing the tick pliers. I had learned why long trousers were an advantage in high weeds. The strategy of drill instructors was now understood and the fact that the use of exercise, as a training aid, still worked on boy scouts was both amusing and enlightening.

We had observed mountain bikers demonstrate exceptional proficiency on their bikes, crossing logs.

I had come to understand that an electronic cookie jar could be as tempting to a youngster as a glass one full of chocolate chip cookies.

We had seen very nice sights and evidence of an old iron industry.

We had been lost and found and I had completed the "loose ends", maps 5 and 6, and my "end to end" hike of the Horse-Shoe Trail.

So ended day 18 on the Horse-Shoe Trail. It was a great hike!

Chapter 22

Reflections of End to End
on the
Horse-Shoe Trail

From Valley Forge to the Appalachian Trail I had actually walked this beautiful, historic, trail after more than 20 years since first thinking about it. The most compelling thought which occurs to me after completing this experience is that I should have done this when the children were younger and taken them along. For hundreds of reasons there was never time, and for hundreds of even better reasons I should have made the time.

I am delighted and blessed to have spent seven days and two nights, of the total 18 days and two nights that it took to complete this hike, in the company of my children, wife, daughter-in-law, and friends. I am also delighted for the time I spent alone on this trail, quietly reflecting on many issues and value judgements that I have made in my lifetime. The experience brought a sense of personal continuity as the "loose ends" from many years ago came into perspective with each observation along the trail.

Insights into many things which were never understood before came with every mile or so. For example, the difference between walking to school and taking the bus was the difference between understanding how a house was built from the ground up rather than having the impression that houses magically appeared in a finished state. Many life events are better understood when they are observed at two or three miles per hour than 55 or 65 miles per hour. Admittedly, some events are better experienced at the higher rate of passing, but now I understand the difference.

The power of a first impression is brought home by spending less than five minutes with people met along the trail. We tell our children about first impressions and how this is valuable. The "up close and personal," as our daughter Renee would say, experience of meeting numerous people for the first time is unique. Generally, each encounter with a person on this hike was one of meeting a new person for the first time. I was amazed at how good the impressions were!

Many people I have talked with who have not hiked this trail, or any trail, are concerned with personal safety. It is always good to be concerned with personal safety and to take measures to avoid increasing the risk of harm to one's self and companions. It is also worth putting the risk in perspective. The people I met and talked with were very nice, and there were hundreds of them. These hundreds of "good news" stories don't make the newspaper headlines or the noon news. Every gruesome news story, by contrast, is broadcast on just about every electronic and print media available. If there is one bad story, pick one from the media, it seems like it was next door because of the extensive media coverage. The world is not as bad as it appears on the front page or the noon news, most of the time. On the other hand, if you are the one that some freak of nature decides to make their victim, the world is a very cruel and brutal place, regardless of where, when or how this happens. By taking some reasonable precautions, everyone can have a good time taking a hike with a comfortable level of safety. Don't be reckless and don't antagonize the wild life or the wild people, but don't become paranoid to the point where you never leave the house either. Someone once told me that generally what I would leave alone would also leave me alone. There is merit in this simple advice.

Labor to establish and maintain the Horse-Shoe Trail in the relatively good state and mostly well marked condition it is in does not happen by chance. I learned that thousands of hours of volunteer labor go into trail maintenance each year. Organized, club sanctioned, working hikes or rides, are a good and very safe way for those who are concerned about being on the trail alone to experience some of the benefits of the trail and companionship with others at the same time. There is always work to be done and helping hands are appreciated according to Horse-Shoe Trail Club members I have spoken with. Get involved.

The amount of maintenance required to repair wear and tear from bicycles and horses is between ten and twenty times, respectively, greater than that to maintain areas where only foot traffic passes, according to the same sources. Inversely, hikers who "leave only footprints" provide most of the volunteer labor with the other travelers not as well represented on maintenance work as their degree of wear would seem to warrant. Let' work together to preserve this common resource.

Boy Scouts and Boy Scout projects were highly visible along the entire trail. Most of the trail which was not on roads in Dauphin County was either in State Game Lands or an Eagle Scout Project on the property of the Milton Hershey School. Scouts were directing the marathon runners in support of Special Olympics west of PA Route 10 as a community service. Just beyond PA Route 501 the Horse-Shoe Trail runs through the Camp Mack Boy Scout Reservation and the scouts do maintenance work there. The Girl Scouts were also noted, not favorably, for their purported dislocation of the Horse-Shoe Trail onto the pavement at Girl Scout Road.

State Game Lands and state and national park lands carry a large number of miles of the Horse-Shoe Trail and are commended for this. I did, and will attempt to continue to, purchase a hunting license every year whether I actually hunt or not as long as the lands are available to walk through and enjoy for recreational hikes. I don't want to see habitat destroyed by undisciplined use, but I felt welcome in the game lands while staying on the designated corridor and truly enjoyed the opportunity to walk through these often wild and always beautiful natural areas. If you are a user of the game lands, please purchase a hunting license or make an effort to support other public use land purchases or projects.

Change is continuous along the Horse-Shoe Trail. Every day every foot of the trail changes, as do the temperatures, views, smells, wildlife, birds, people, insects and the total environment. In some cases this is gradual and predictable, in other cases it is sudden and surprising. In some areas the trail, and the corridor it runs through, are seriously threatened by land use practices. There is opportunity to have nice walking trails, highways and developments which co-exist. Make an effort to help this happen. There is high community value in a walking corridor which is much more obvious to me after the experience of walking this trail.

A map, functional compass and trail guide were indispensable. Maps and trail guides are available from:

Horse-Shoe Trail Club Inc.
P.O. Box 182
Birchrunville, PA 19421-0182,

as well as from many local sporting goods stores and outfitters. The latter also will have a compass.

Trail guides are supplemented by the "Blaze", the official newsletter of the Horse-Shoe Trail Club. This publication provides information on organized hikes, trail maintenance outings, and trail relocations. It was worth the price of joining just to have this information. If you are interested in hiking or horseback riding, consider joining the club and supporting the trail.

Finally, the absolute minimum amount of litter along more than a hundred miles of trail was truly amazing! The abundant amount of debris, litter and garbage dumped along highways and rural roads was also sadly amazing. I urge those traveling the highways and byways to be more careful to place their debris in a proper receptacle, and hope public agencies will develop programs to clean up the roads a little better. I commend those who pack out what they take in, and perhaps an item or two which someone has dropped, leaving only foot or hoof prints. Keep up this outstanding example of stewardship.

New Commissioners took office in Dauphin County during the writing of this book. Perhaps they will improve the conditions noted regarding dumping and watershed pollution along the northern sections of the trail in Dauphin County.

Take the Kids and take some friends. With a little common sense, the Horse-Shoe Trail, away from the roads, is a relatively safe, fascinating, and friendly place to spend a day or a vacation.

It was a great idea to take a hike! It took 18 days and two nights to complete the Horse-Shoe Trail from end to end on a part time basis and it was a great experience. Stronger hikers, with better endurance, can probably complete the trail in much less time. For the horseback riders, I was told it takes a week on horseback without pushing too hard. I enjoyed hiking on the Horse-Shoe Trail and the folks I met along the way. I hope you will "take a hike" and enjoy the experience also.

Mike Pavelek II